MW01193975

THE RIVETING STORY OF
SOPHAL UNG

ALMIGHTY IS HIS NAME

RANDY CLARK
with SUSAN THOMPSON

CHARISMA
HOUSE

Most CHARISMA HOUSE BOOK GROUP products are available at special quantity discounts for bulk purchase for sales promotions, premiums, fund-raising, and educational needs. For details, write Charisma House Book Group, 600 Rinehart Road, Lake Mary, Florida 32746, or telephone (407) 333-0600.

ALMIGHTY IS HIS NAME
  by Randy Clark With Susan Thompson
Published by Charisma House
Charisma Media/Charisma House Book Group
600 Rinehart Road
Lake Mary, Florida 32746
www.charismahouse.com

This book or parts thereof may not be reproduced in any form, stored in a retrieval system, or transmitted in any form by any means—electronic, mechanical, photocopy, recording, or otherwise—without prior written permission of the publisher, except as provided by United States of America copyright law.

Unless otherwise noted, all Scripture quotations are from the Holy Bible, New International Version®, NIV®. Copyright © 1973, 1978, 1984, 2011 by Biblica, Inc.™ Used by permission of Zondervan. All rights reserved worldwide. www.zondervan.com. The "NIV" and "New International Version" are trademarks registered in the United States Patent and Trademark Office by Biblica, Inc.™

Scripture quotations marked MEV are taken from the Holy Bible, Modern English Version. Copyright © 2014 by Military Bible Association. Used by permission. All rights reserved.

Copyright © 2016 by Randy Clark and Susan Thompson
All rights reserved

Cover design by Lisa Rae McClure
Design Director: Justin Evans

Visit the author's website at http://globalawakening.com/.

Library of Congress Cataloging-in-Publication Data:
An application to register this book for cataloging has been
submitted to the Library of Congress.
International Standard Book Number: 978-1-62998-632-6
E-book ISBN: 978-1-62998-633-3

While the author has made every effort to provide accurate
Internet addresses at the time of publication, neither the
publisher nor the author assumes any responsibility for
errors or for changes that occur after publication.

First edition

16 17 18 19 20 — 987654321
Printed in the United States of America

Arise, shine, for your light has come,
and the glory of the LORD rises upon you.
See, darkness covers the earth
and thick darkness is over the peoples,
but the LORD rises upon you
and his glory appears over you.
Nations will come to your light,
and kings to the brightness of your dawn.

—ISAIAH 60:1–3

PUBLISHER'S NOTE

THIS BOOK IS the firsthand testimony of Cambodian pastor Sophal Ung. Sophal gave this testimony to Randy Clark during a series of interviews, which Randy and his team videotaped. The transcripts of the video interviews were sent to Susan Thompson, and she was tasked with transforming them into a book. She has taken great care to maintain the integrity of Sophal's testimony throughout by writing in his "voice" and being mindful not to change or embellish details. We believe readers will find Sophal's testimony to be a significant addition to the great body of testimonies that have come to us down through the ages that give witness to the unfailing love and mercy of God. To Him be the glory!

CONTENTS

PART THREE
THE CAMPS

PART FOUR
AMERICA

PART FIVE
RETURN TO CAMBODIA

PART SIX
A NEW SEASON

PREFACE

THE COUNTRY OF Cambodia is located on the Indochina peninsula of Southeast Asia, bordered by Vietnam to the east, Laos to the northeast, Thailand to the northwest, and the Gulf of Thailand to the southwest. With a population of approximately fifteen million people, according to a 2013 census, Cambodia struggles with political corruption, widespread poverty, and the scars of war and genocide.

The recorded history of Cambodia dates back to the third millennium BC, when rice farmers from the north migrated into the area. European missionaries visited Cambodia in the sixteenth century, and by the nineteenth century the country had become a French protectorate, part of French Indochina. In 1953 Cambodia won its independence from France under the strong rule of King Norodom Sihanouk, who ruled the country until 1970 when he was deposed by General Lon Nol and Cambodia's National Assembly.

The Khmer Rouge, followers of the Communist Party of Kampuchea and an offshoot of the Vietnam People's Army of North Vietnam, emerged in Cambodia in the 1970s as the war in Vietnam spilled across the border. They controlled Cambodia from 1975 to 1979, when they were defeated by pro-Vietnamese, communist occupation forces. In 1991 Cambodia was officially recognized as a nation-state by the United Nations–sponsored Paris Peace Agreement.

The Khmer Rouge, led by the ruthless socialist revolutionary Pol Pot—and fueled by the writings of Vladimir Lenin and Karl Marx, as well as by the French Communist Party and Maoism ideology—carried out large-scale ethnic cleansing. They annihilated millions of Cambodians and displaced the Khmer people in what some modern-day historians refer to as the Cambodian Diaspora. The foundation of Cambodian society was systematically destroyed as ethnic minorities and ethnic Khmer who were considered a threat—including intellectuals, professionals, the rich, and former government and military authorities—were slaughtered by the hundreds of thousands along with their families.

Under the Khmer Rouge, considered by historians to be one of the most brutal regimes in history, an estimated two million people died from disease, starvation, execution, or forced-labor exhaustion during its short, four-year reign.

From 1975 to 1978 Vietnamese communists and Khmer Rouge forces fought each other across Cambodia, with much of the fighting centered in and around the capital, Phnom Penh. The Vietnamese gained control of the city in January 1979 and ousted the Khmer Rouge. Throughout the 1980s Vietnamese military and civilian forces united to restore Cambodia's economy and resist the Khmer Rouge.

The 1991 Paris Peace Agreement officially marked the end of the Vietnamese-Cambodian War and opened the door to repatriation of the displaced Khmer civilians. Factional armies were disarmed and demobilized, enabling the groundwork for a democratic election process to take shape. A multiparty democracy built on the framework of a constitutional monarchy was established as a result of elections and continues to rule Cambodia today; however, the situation is far from ideal. Democracy is fragile in Cambodia, with widespread political corruption and grinding poverty plaguing the country as it continues to struggle with the physical and psychological scars of war.

Christians in Cambodia today make up about 2 percent of the population. Estimates are that during the Khmer Rouge regime approximately 80 percent of Cambodian Christians were executed on the killing fields. Since that time a small band of believers that numbered about two thousand has grown significantly into the Christian church that exists today in Cambodia, a nation that is still predominantly Buddhist.

It is against this backdrop of upheaval that the story of Sophal Ung unfolds.

—SUSAN THOMPSON
EDITOR

INTRODUCTION

I FIRST MET SOPHAL Ung in 2003 in Phnom Penh, Cambodia, while in the city with a ministry team conducting a conference for Vietnamese pastors. I originally came to know Sophal through his daughter Martha and her husband, Michael Ho. Michael and Martha came to the Toronto Blessing in 1994, during their honeymoon. For those who are not familiar with it, the Toronto Blessing is a mighty outpouring of the Holy Spirit that began in a small church—the Toronto Airport Vineyard Church in Ontario, Canada in 1994 when God called me there to preach. What was supposed to be four nights of preaching exploded into nightly meetings that by 1995 saw thousands in attendance each evening and continue to this day. The Toronto Blessing began as renewal, as the Holy Spirit did a deep work in the hearts of all who came. Eventually the fires of revival began to burn resulting in numerical church growth around the globe.

I was preaching the day Martha and Michael Ho came to Toronto. Afterward, as I began to work my way down the long prayer line that snaked around the perimeter of the sanctuary, the power of God was strong, and many people were unable to stand as they encountered His presence. I came upon a young Asian couple in the prayer line, and as I prayed for them, they too fell down under the power of God. Moving to the next person in line I heard myself say, "May what happened in the book *Anointed for Burial**come upon this couple." Immediately Michael rose from the floor and shouted to me: "Martha's father is one of the main characters in that book!" His words stopped me in my tracks. I returned to the young couple and began to pray fervently for the Father's love to envelop them.

The next night I called Martha to the podium to share her experience from the previous evening. As she opened her mouth to speak, the tangible presence of God came over her again. She later told me it felt like a huge, thick weight pressing upon her. Again she fell to the floor, where she remained for the next several hours, shaking uncontrollably in the presence of God. She experienced a powerful baptism of

---

* Todd and DeAnn Burke, *Anointed for Burial* (Plainfield, NJ: Bridge Logos, 1977). This is the story of the Burkes' missionary time in Cambodia in the early 1970s. It was through the Burkes' church in Phnom Penh that Sophal Ung came to Christ after God healed him on his deathbed.

God's love as He gave her visions of lost and destitute orphans.

During her time of intimacy with the Lord Martha received God's healing for the rejection and abandonment she had experienced while separated from her parents during the Khmer Rouge occupation of Cambodia, when she was just three years old.

"To experience the raw power of His redeeming work on the cross was both extremely painful and freeing," Martha said. "I wept and shook for maybe three hours while soaking in His presence. This was the beginning of my healing process, which led to deliverance and a greater hunger for God."

This encounter with Martha and Michael in Toronto in 1994 led to a meeting with Sophal Ung when I was in Cambodia nine years later, in 2003. This book is the result of a series of interviews I conducted with Sophal in 2010. It took another two years to have the interviews transcribed so that this book could be written.

I believe Sophal Ung is one of the greatest apostles in the nation of Cambodia today. His heart burns for the salvation of his country. When he visited the Toronto Blessing, he experienced a powerful new filling of the Holy Spirit that affected his entire body. He shook and trembled under the power of the Spirit, with movements similar to those that resulted when the Vietnamese tortured him with electrical prods. But this time, instead of bringing weakness and pain, the shaking and trembling brought him joy, strength, and boldness as God's power filled him. After this experience Sophal began to reach out to Cambodians in the United States who were considering returning to Cambodia to minister. He encouraged them to go with him to Toronto first and receive from God.

What you are about to read in these pages is taken from Sophal's extended testimony just as it was told to me. During our talks Sophal did not reveal much emotion, as is typical of those raised in an Asian culture—with the exception coming during our tour of the prison where he was held. Though I understand that his reserved nature is partly cultural, I have come to see Sophal as a man not interested in revealing himself—his greatest desire is to reveal Jesus Christ.

Sophal is an amazing man, and his story will give you great hope for the advancement of the kingdom of God on the earth. Like I did, you will find yourself alternating between praising God for His goodness and weeping over the depravity of man's sinful nature as you read Sophal's firsthand account of life in Cambodia during the most turbulent period in that country's history.

Born into a devout Buddhist family in an overwhelmingly Buddhist nation, Sophal began his journey with Christ in the 1970s, in a church planted in Phnom Penh by American missionaries Todd and DeAnn Burke. The Burkes came to Cambodia in 1973, during the final days of Cambodia's last regime before the Khmer Rouge government took power. They were forced to evacuate in 1975 and never returned. However, the church they left behind provided a foundation for Christianity in Cambodia that has been built upon by many and remains in force today. Their story is chronicled in the book *Anointed for Burial.*

During the Khmer Rouge occupation, millions of Cambodians were imprisoned, starved, beaten, tortured, and put to death in the killing fields. The depravity of the killing fields rivaled that of the Nazi concentration camps of World War II, with Khmer soldiers ripping infants from their mothers' arms and throwing them into the air to use as target practice. The average age of a Khmer Rouge soldier was fifteen. The hideous genocide did not end when the Khmer Rouge were driven out by the Vietnamese communists. Intolerant of any threat to their fledgling communist government in Cambodia, the Vietnamese continued to imprison, torture, and kill political prisoners—and anyone else they considered a threat to communism.

Sophal was imprisoned by the Vietnamese communist government in the early 1980s. Captured by soldiers on a dark road one night as he came home from visiting a friend, he spent more than three years in prison and suffered greatly at the hands of the communist soldiers. Of the estimated seventeen thousand people Sophal knew of who were thrown in prison during the time he was there, only seven survived.

Before the war Cambodia had a population of approximately 7.89 million. Of those, an estimated 25 percent died at the hands of the Khmer Rouge.

During my time in Cambodia with Sophal, he took me to the prison where he spent some of his darkest days. It is now called Tuol Sleng Genocide Museum but once was Chao Ponhea Yat High School. Democratic Kampuchea (the Khmer Rouge state that ruled Cambodia from 1975 to 1979) divided up the classrooms into individual cells on the first floor while reserving the second floor for mass detention. Dense barbed wire surrounded the building where thousands of peasants, workers, technicians, engineers, doctors, teachers, students, Buddhist monks, ministers, soldiers from all ranks of the Cambodian Democratic corps, and foreigners were imprisoned and exterminated along with their families.

As we toured the prison together, evidence of torture was still visible everywhere. Instruments of torture; dossiers and documents; and lists of prisoners' names, their mug shots, and their clothing and belongings are now housed in the museum. Mass graves surround the facility, but most are located about fifteen kilometers southwest of Phnom Penh in the village of Choeung Ek, in the Dangkor district, Kandal Province.

Sophal explained to me how prisoners spent their time when not being tortured. With their hands chained together and their feet chained in wooden stocks, they could do nothing but lie in their cells. Many cells measured only 2.6 feet by 6.5 feet, making it impossible to stand or sit. If you wanted to eat your daily ration of rice and water, you had to eat like a dog.

Torture didn't stop when the sun went down. The nights were pierced by the sounds of screaming as prisoners had their nails ripped from their hands and feet. Torture by beating, electrocution, and cutting went on around the clock. Sometimes prisoners with their hands and feet bound would be hung upside down and their heads shoved into buckets of water. When they would pass out, buckets of liquid chemical fertilizer would be poured over their heads to revive them.

Many of the cells in the museum had pictures of the swollen, bruised, and battered bodies of prisoners. Their blood, which had covered the walls and floors, was still visible. When the Khmer Rouge abandoned the prison and fled before the advancing Vietnamese army, the prison was left unattended and isolated for some time before the Vietnamese discovered it. They found the prison by following the stench of dead bodies.

The few people who managed to survive were so emaciated that they were almost unrecognizable—their hair long and matted with blood and filth. When Sophal finally escaped from prison, his daughters were so shocked at his appearance that they ran away, terrified by their first sight of him.

Our tour of the prison together was very emotional. Many times Sophal was overcome, weeping until he could regain his composure. His one consolation in all he suffered while imprisoned is the knowledge that, before they died, many of his fellow prisoners came to Christ as a result of his efforts to bring the lifesaving message of the gospel into that darkest of places.

But the prison was not the only place where God used Sophal. His story stretches far beyond those walls. It reaches across the city of Phnom Penh, into the countryside, through the killing fields and jungles, into the refugee camps on the Thai border, and eventually to America. It is a story of a special kind of courage found in the heart of a man whose faith in his Lord and Savior, Jesus Christ, never wavered even in the face of unbelievably overwhelming odds.

Sophal's steadfast faithfulness to the message of the gospel has yielded enormous fruit for the kingdom of God. Hundreds of churches have been planted as a result of his efforts, both in Cambodia and in America. He has trained countless leaders, fed orphans, housed and clothed the poor and displaced, and seen miracle upon miracle as the hand of God has stayed the enemy while reaching out to heal a broken people. It is my great privilege to help Sophal Ung share his story with the world.

Mankind has always searched for heroes, for someone to come and save us from our own wickedness. Two thousand years ago God sent His Son into the world to be the Savior of all humanity. Sophal Ung knows Jesus Christ, the Savior, and has served Him with a courage and dignity that should be the goal of all who call themselves beloved of God.

—RANDY CLARK, DMin, ThD
OVERSEER OF THE APOSTOLIC NETWORK
OF GLOBAL AWAKENING

In the early 1980s when I was a young wife and mother in Herndon, Virginia, a friend gave me a copy of Corrie ten Boom's book *The Hiding Place*. This story of a watchmaker and his family in Holland who suffered for their faith in the midst of the Holocaust deeply touched my heart. I have read many outstanding books since then, but few have impacted me quite like Corrie ten Boom's book until I read Sophal Ung's story. I wept the first time I edited it, and it continued to touch my heart even as I completed the final edits. There is something so deep about the way in which the heart of a person responds to the love of Jesus in the midst of unrestrained evil, and the way in which Jesus answers. He wants our heart. When we give it to Him unconditionally, the kingdom of God comes with a love that denies no one.

—SUSAN THOMPSON
EDITOR

PART ONE

THE EARLY
YEARS

CHAPTER 1

I WAS BORN INTO a Buddhist family in a small village in the southern province of Takéo, Cambodia. At that time about 99 percent of the population of Cambodia was Buddhist.

Christianity began to make inroads into Cambodia in the mid-1800s, under French colonization, with the arrival of Roman Catholic missionaries. Almost a century later, in 1923, the Christian and Missionary Alliance brought Protestant missionaries to Cambodia. In the 1970s two American missionaries, Todd and DeAnn Burke, led my brother Samoeum to Christ, and it was through the efforts of Samoeum that I too became a Christian.

I had no knowledge of Christianity growing up. My father was a Buddhist leader in our village, and everyone in our village was a devout Buddhist.

When I was about six or seven years old, my father sent me to live at the temple with the monks, as was the custom for young Buddhist boys. I lived at the temple for a few years before returning home to my family. Between ages fifteen and eighteen every boy had to give another two years of his life in the temple as a monk before he could go on to high school or college. Many remained to become lifelong monks. It was my father's desire that I become a monk. Following tradition, I was sent back to live at the temple when I was fifteen.

I was very unhappy with my parents' decision. The austere life of a monk held no appeal for me. I didn't know what to do. I didn't know Jesus, so I just talked to the sky and the wind. And then one day I came up with a plan. With the help of my younger brother, who brought my suitcase to me, I slipped out of the temple in the early-morning hours and caught a bus to Phnom Penh. I had no idea where I was going or what I was going to do when I got there, but at least I wasn't going to be a monk.

ORPHANED

One thing I did know was that my decision meant I had gone against Cambodian culture. A disobedient child brought great disgrace to the family, often resulting in disinheritance. When children are disinherited from their family, they can lose their family name. Often families would make disinheritance public by publishing a notice in the newspaper. When my dad discovered that I had escaped, in anger and shame he cut me off from the family. I was rejected and disinherited and lost my family name. I became an orphan.

When I arrived in Phnom Penh, I knew no one. I was a fifteen-year-old boy alone in a large city with nothing but a small suitcase. Not knowing where to go, I stayed in the bus station for three days. I might have lived in that bus station for a lot longer had it not been for a Chinese boy and the kindness of his family. This young boy noticed me at the bus station, and when he learned that I was an orphan, he invited me to his house. I was able to live with this Chinese family and go to school.

To make money for my school tuition, I sold newspapers. I would collect my papers in the morning, deliver some to houses in the neighborhood, and sell the rest on the streets. I lived like this until I graduated from high school at age eighteen. Unable to find employment anywhere else, I went to work in a restaurant. My time in the restaurant proved invaluable, as I would later own my own restaurants.

My first introduction to Christianity came in 1968. Someone invited me to church to hear the good news about Jesus. Being a very lonely young man, I accepted the invitation to attend church, but it would be many years before I would accept Jesus's invitation to surrender my heart and life to Him.

WAR ARRIVES

In the 1970s the Khmer Rouge began taking over parts of the countryside in Cambodia while also attacking the capital, Phnom Penh. War raged and fighting ravaged the country. In 1975 the Khmer Rouge managed to take Phnom Penh. General Lon Nol became president, replacing Cambodia's King Norodom Sihanouk, who had escaped to exile in China.

Vietnamese refugees who had fled into Cambodia during the Vietnam War were forced to return home when General Lon became president. They were given two weeks to sell their homes and all their belongings and leave the country. I was able to capitalize on this mass exodus by buying up at very cheap prices what the Vietnamese were selling and reselling it at a profit. I made a lot of money and became a prosperous businessman. At one point I owned three restaurants and a taxi company, and worked as a journalist.

As the Khmer Rouge advanced on Phnom Penh, the fighting grew fierce. The city was bombed nightly. I had an apartment near the Mekong River at the time. Every night scores of people were killed during the bombing raids. Everyone was very fearful, and many fled the city. I was afraid but didn't know where to go.

As a wealthy businessman, I had a lot of friends in the city. One day we gathered together to talk about how we could escape the country and where we would go. A number of us knew President Nol's younger brother. We contacted him and were granted permission to leave, but the price was very high to fly us out of Cambodia to the Thai border. Thankfully I had the money and hastily made arrangements to fly myself and eight family members out of the country the next day. In all there were twenty-eight of us who planned to leave with our families. We were told to go to the American Embassy at seven o'clock the next morning, where helicopters would be waiting to fly us to Thailand.

That night we decided to celebrate. Gathering together, my friends and I partied until about eleven o'clock, and then, while the rest of my friends left for home, I stayed behind to help clean up. Within an hour, all twenty-seven of them were dead—killed in a bombing raid on the city. Had I not stayed to clean up, I too would have died that night.

Fear overtook me at that point, and I fled to hide in the basement of my house. For hours I paced back and forth, praying to every god I could think of. I stayed in that basement for three days, until the bombing stopped. I didn't know what to do. Then one night I slipped and fell in the bathroom, hitting my head. The fall was a bad one. It knocked me unconscious, and I went into a coma. For three months I was unconscious, on a ventilator, and clinging to life. The doctors could do nothing for me.

When it seemed evident that my death was imminent, my family was notified to come to pay their last respects. Despite having disowned me, they came. They prayed to their gods, offered sacrifices, and brought in all kinds of doctors; but no one could help me as I lay dying in my bed, tethered to life support. But God in His mercy had plans for me that I knew nothing about. I didn't even know God then, but He knew me, and it wasn't His intention for me to die at that time.

CHAPTER 2

THE WAR AND its hideous carnage had stirred the hearts of the Christian church for Cambodia, and God began to work through American missionaries Todd and DeAnn Burke. The Burkes had been called to Cambodia in 1973, to take over the work of missionaries Larry and Jean Romans. When Phnom Penh fell, the embassies closed, and all foreigners were ordered to leave the country. Todd and DeAnn were told to leave, but they refused. Cambodia was now their home, not America, and they were determined to stay. Even the embassy's warning that they could be killed did not deter them.

The Burkes were granted permission to remain in Cambodia for a time. Their efforts to plant a church began with evening English classes, which were really house-church services, as they were with many other missionaries. Within a short time, about 150 people were attending the Burkes' class, and that number quickly mushroomed to 300 people. My younger brother Samoeum was one of them.

If you remember, Samoeum was the one who had helped me escape the Buddhist monastery. Because of my disobedience, he had been forced by our father to become a monk in my stead. Word reached Samoeum about the English classes at a church in Phnom Penh, and God sovereignly touched his heart to attend. The Khmer Rouge had closed the roads from our small village to Phnom Penh, but as a monk, Samoeum was allowed to travel.

He arrived in the city, and within a few weeks of starting English classes, he was powerfully touched by God. Leaving Buddhism behind, he accepted Jesus into his heart. In the ensuing months and years, God anointed Samoeum in worship and evangelism, making him a mighty force for God's kingdom in Cambodia. It was Samoeum whom God used to bring me to Christ.

When word of my desperate medical condition reached Samoeum, he traveled to my house to pay his last respects. Before returning to Phnom Penh, he photographed me, and when he was back in the city, he put my picture on the wall in the prayer room at the Burkes' church. That Friday night they began to pray for me. Their prayers continued into the morning hours. At one point Samoeum stood and put his hands on my picture. As he did, a young prophetess named

NaredNareth, who was just sixteen years old, received a word of knowledge. God told her that Samoeum was to return to my house and pray for me. God gave her very specific details about where my house was located and about my condition, details that she had no earthly knowledge of.

"When you pray for your brother, God will heal him," NaredNareth said to Samoeum.

THE GLORY OF GOD

Knowing my parents would be with me and that he would encounter resistance because of their Buddhist beliefs, Samoeum returned to my house with a team from the church. Standing beside my bed, he turned to my father and asked if they could pray for me.

"How are you going to pray?" asked my father. "We have been praying for many days, and Sophal's condition has not improved."

"Your prayers have not worked because you have been praying to Buddha," Samoeum said. "I tell you, when we pray to God, Jesus will heal him."

Then Samoeum began to share with my parents that he no longer practiced Buddhism but was now a follower of Jesus Christ. They were so desperate for my healing that they agreed to listen to him, but my dad said, "If your God does not heal Sophal, I will throw you out the window!"

Samoeum began to read the Bible and share the gospel, and as he did, hope came upon my parents. Then he prayed for me as the others on the team accompanied his prayers with singing and worship. They prayed over me and worshipped throughout the night and into the early hours of the morning. At five o'clock in the morning I woke up for the first time in three months.

As I lay there in bed, I heard beautiful voices singing, voices unlike anything I had ever heard before. And then my eyes opened, and I saw the manifest glory of God come into the room. It was shining with many colors, almost like a rainbow. The colors were indescribable, like thousands of different-colored lights brightly glistening. I had a hard time keeping my eyes open because of the brilliance of God's presence. Some years later, while ministering in the prisons, I would see this same glory cloud come into our midst.

HEALED

As Samoeum knelt in prayer for me, I motioned for him to come close. As he did, I saw the glory and goodness of God all over him and all over the entire team of young people with him.

"Jesus loves you," Samoeum said to me. "Jesus has just healed you, right now."

Upon hearing this I began to cry. No one had ever told me that I was loved. For many years my father had denied and rejected me, judging me to the point of disowning me. I had suffered so much heartache. Since age fifteen I had been an orphan. But on the day

Samoeum told me Jesus loved me, it was like a bomb went off in my heart; it just exploded with joy.

We laughed and hugged and wept together. Samoeum kept telling me how much Jesus loved me and that He had healed me. He told me about the words of knowledge God had given NaredNareth that had caused him to return to my house and pray for my healing.

We spent the morning talking together, until exhaustion overtook everyone and they went off to other parts of the house to rest. But I couldn't rest. I hadn't eaten for three months and I was starving. The doctors had told my family that if I did come out of the coma I would not be able to eat right away. They said my digestive system would not handle food. In fact, they said it could be life-threatening for me to eat anything.

Everyone else was asleep, and I knew they would not help me to the kitchen even if they were awake, so I simply asked God for help. Lying there in bed, I began to thank God for healing me and asked Him to get me into the kitchen. "Father, I need to eat—now," I said. "Please help me walk to the kitchen."

I was very frail. It took me about fifteen minutes to cross from the bedroom to the kitchen in my pitiful condition. But what joy greeted me when I arrived. My family had cooked a lot of food, and I immediately claimed it. Pulling up a chair, I began to eat.

I sampled some soup and then waited a few minutes. Nothing happened, so I began to eat again. I had one bowl of food, waited a few minutes, then ate another bowl, and so on until I was full. I was so frail that I couldn't get up and make it back to bed, so I just sat on a stool in the kitchen, and that is where my mom found me when she woke up. Alarmed that I had eaten so much, she immediately called the doctor.

"Sophal! You're going to die from eating too soon!" my mother wailed.

"Mother, I'm not dying," I said. "I'm just full and need help getting back to bed."

When the doctor arrived, he too proceeded to tell me that I was going to die from eating too soon.

"No, I am not going to die," I repeated. "God healed me, and I'm going to live!"

I was so frail, it was a week before I could walk again. During that time my father lovingly carried me wherever I needed to go, until my legs regained their strength.

COMING TO CHRIST

Because of my healing, my parents wanted to hear more about this Christian God. They agreed to come to the Burkes' church with Samoeum. The church sent a big van to my house to pick up everyone. My parents and another brother, my aunt and uncle, and my eighty-one-year-old grandmother all piled into the van. There were eighteen of us in all who went to church that day. They put us on the front row, and Todd preached about the love of God and the father heart of God. Then came the altar call.

"If there is anyone here today who has sin in their life and needs to repent, please come to the front," Todd said.

I ran up to the front and fell on my face on the floor. My father, my mother, and my grandmother came to the front too. We didn't know what to say; we didn't know anything yet. It was our first time in church. As we lay there, Pastor Burke told us how much Jesus loved us and that Jesus had healed me. I began to cry, and so did my father.

"Son, I love you," my father said. "I love you! Please forgive me for what happened."

"I love you too, Father," I cried.

Suddenly the Holy Spirit came and hit everyone in that church, knocking them all to the floor. A revival ensued, and many Buddhists gave their lives to the Lord as a result of that visitation of the Holy Spirit.

CHAPTER 3

M Y HOUSE WAS so full of darkness and evil from all the idols and sacrifices offered up to Buddha during my illness that I didn't want to go back there to recuperate. I asked if I could stay at the Burkes' church instead. My father wanted to stay at the church too.

They put me upstairs in the third-floor prayer room. It was just the right place for me. It was to that room that they would bring those who were too sick to walk. We would pray over them, and God would heal them. Miracles happened all the time in that room. It was the perfect place for me to heal and to see what God was doing. My faith grew enormously during that time.

As the war raged, God poured out His Spirit on the people of Cambodia, moving powerfully through the work of the Burkes' church in Phnom Penh. When I was well enough, I joined the Burkes in their efforts.

At one point the church felt led to hold a crusade. We were granted permission to use an indoor stadium in the city. About a thousand people came. There were many healings, and as word of the healings spread, people began trying to come in from the outlying provinces, but most couldn't make it. Travel was difficult, and the people were very poor.

The sick who couldn't make it into the city began to send their pictures to the church along with their prayer requests for healing. We would put the pictures up on the walls of our prayer room and then go around the room laying hands on the pictures, asking God to heal each person. We eventually had thousands of pictures on the walls. Testimonies of healing filtered back to us as God opened the eyes of the blind and the lame walked. Even those who had been born blind or lame were healed.

Our prayer room was open 24/7. God's anointing on the church and the Burkes' work was strong. There were those whom God anointed for healing, those He anointed for prophecy, and some He anointed for deliverance.

I remember the day one of our Cambodian pastors came to pray. It was early in the morning. As he knelt in prayer, NaredNareth, the prophetess, spoke to him. She was not one to hold back when the Lord revealed something to her, even people's sins. I know that is not how we teach people to operate in the prophetic today, but that is how she operated. If you had secret sins, it was better not to come into the prayer room when NaredNareth was there.

She was sitting and weeping when this pastor entered, and she began to pray. Never looking up, she pointed to him and said, "Nou-Thai, before you come into this holy room, you go home and fix things with your wife. Forgive each other, and then you can come back to this room and pray." Startled, Nou-Thai got up and left the church. Knowing that he had just heard from God, he immediately went home, found his wife, and asked for her forgiveness.

BAPTIZED IN THE SPIRIT

About three months after I was saved, I received the baptism of the Holy Spirit. It happened one night in the prayer room. The prayer room was a quiet place. Those who came in would fall silent before the Lord so that all could hear the voice of the Lord clearly and without distraction.

Everyone had been fasting and praying that particular day. I was sitting next to NaredNareth when heat began to come over my entire body. It went from the top of my head to my feet, and it happened quickly. I began to shake violently as the power of God came upon me. My brother tried to quiet me but could not. I was shaking so hard and I was so hot that I became a distraction to the others in the room who were trying to pray.

I was escorted from the prayer room to the baptismal room. There was a big tub of water in the room. Because I was burning hot, they put me in the tub. They left me there, locking the gate as they went out. The water was cool when they first put me in, but it quickly became hot. I could see the water starting to bubble around me.

"Get me out of here, Samoeum!" I cried. "This water is boiling hot!"

After much shouting, my brother finally came and unlocked the door, but he kept telling me, "Sophal, you are acting crazy."

Suddenly I physically saw a huge hand holding me. I was shaking so hard, I couldn't walk. My knees were knocking, and I couldn't stand up. The huge hand took me from the baptismal room into the prayer room and put me down right in the middle of the room where about three hundred people were gathered in prayer.

Under a powerful anointing of the Holy Spirit, I began to speak in tongues. I spent the entire night in this condition in the Spirit, with the Lord speaking to me. Many of those around me were writing things down. I don't know everything I said during that time, but somehow the pastors and leaders were able to write down some of what they heard.

At one point God gave me a vision. I saw an entire city burning with fire. Then I saw a dark color like blackness cover the whole of Cambodia. Later I would understand this vision—when Cambodia burned with the fire of war and then fell into great darkness under the communists. Under the Vietnamese communist government that occupied Cambodia after the fall of the Khmer Rouge, the Christian church in Cambodia remained underground until 1990, when the occupation ended and Christianity was legalized.

After my baptism in the Spirit I was just too Spirit-filled to continue living in the prayer room. My manifestations were a distraction amid the quiet of 24/7 prayers. I was moved to a nearby house where the church had its Bible school. My father and I began to attend the school. For four or five hours every morning we would study at the school, and in the evenings we would go out into the streets and evangelize. Miraculous healings accompanied our street evangelism. So great were the numbers of people who were saved from street evangelism that we were able to open eight house churches during the time we attended the Bible school.

THE CHURCH FLOURISHES

At that time there were some two million people living in Phnom Penh, many of them refugees from the countryside where the Khmer Rouge had taken over. I was not a preacher at that time. I didn't know how to preach or teach, but I did know how to drive a car. My brother and I would put tents in the car and, together with a team, go and find a place to set up.

I remember one day in particular. We had set up our tents and begun to preach. Hundreds of people came. We preached for three nights, and on the third night the authorities came and told my brother to move the tents.

"No!" he replied. "We've spent a lot of time putting these tents up, and we won't take them down!"

In spite of his steadfast refusal to leave, the authorities would not allow us to stay. We were forced to pack up and move on. A few of our people had remained behind to clean up when, suddenly, bombs started falling. The exact spot where our tents had been was bombed. Had we stayed, we all would have been killed that night, along with the hundreds of people who would have come to receive a touch from God.

CHAPTER 4

I WAS NOT A preacher, although I longed in my
heart to preach. I was a good writer, having been
a journalist, but I was not very good at speaking.
After my baptism in the Spirit I began to write songs,
many of which helped bring people to the Lord, but
I still longed to preach. I would listen to my brother
preach. He was very good, and I was jealous of his
abilities. I wanted the anointing to preach too, so I
approached God.

"Father," I said, "here is my younger brother, who
was once a monk, and You have anointed him for
preaching. You know that I am jealous. I want the same
anointing. I want to preach. And I want to lay hands on
people and see them healed."

Up to this point I had not been used to heal others directly, although many around me in the church were being used in that way. I wanted the gift of healing and of preaching, and so I prayed. For three months I spent as much time as possible in the prayer room, but nothing happened. My work for the kingdom was confined to picking up people and driving them to and from church.

Then one night, unknown to me, God spoke to NaredNareth. It was a Saturday night. God told her that I would be the one to preach the sermon in church the next morning. As it happened, that Sunday was the anniversary of our mother church. It seemed everyone else had heard the word that I was to preach except me.

I got up as usual the next day, drove around the city bringing people to the church, and then went and cleaned the bathrooms. By the time I got into the service it was late. The worship was almost over. Dirty from driving and cleaning, I sat along the back wall. As worship came to a close, the worship leader announced, "Before Brother Sophal comes up to share, we have a special song for him." Then he began to play and sing.

Now, there was no one else in the church named Sophal, but I couldn't believe what I was hearing. I sent a young boy up front to the worship leader with a note asking, "Who is Sophal?" The boy came back to me and said, "Sophal Ung, you are preaching today."

I was shocked and embarrassed. My clothes were dirty, and I was totally unprepared, but I also knew that this was what I had been praying for. I had asked God to anoint me to preach and teach and to lay hands on the sick and heal them, and now here He was opening the door for me. The problem wasn't just my dirty clothes; I had no message to preach!

I sent a note back to the worship leader, asking him to continue the worship for a while longer so I could prepare myself. Grabbing my Bible, I headed into the bathroom. Turning on the water full force, I knelt on the floor and, opening my Bible, asked the Lord what He would have me preach. As I turned the pages my eyes fell on John 3:16. The Lord quickened this scripture in my heart at that moment, and I knew then what I was to preach.

"Thank You, Lord!" I cried as I jumped up from the floor.

PREACHING TO THE LOST

With my Bible in my hand, I went out into the main sanctuary and up to the platform. I think there were about six hundred people there that Sunday. I had never stood before such a large group of people, and I began to shake with fear. I was shaking so hard I could barely stand up. Looking over at a group of people near me, I asked them to pray that God would help me. Then I began to sing, and as I sang, people in the congregation began to stand up. Together we worshipped the Lord, and it was powerful.

When the worship ended, silence fell over the church, and I began to preach with boldness about the love of God. It was my first message, but it was filled with the power of God. I preached for a long time. I taught the people about the differences between Jesus and Buddha. Because I had studied Buddhism for six years, I knew what it was all about.

"Jesus is the real God, the King of kings." I said. "Buddha is not God.

"Do you know that God sent Jesus from heaven to earth to die on the cross for our sins?" I asked them.

Then I gave an altar call. All eighteen of the Buddhist monks my father had brought to church that day came forward and knelt on the floor at the front. It was a mighty miracle of God. I was so excited, I began to dance, and as I danced I heard the audible voice of God. It was the first time I had heard His voice audibly, and it was very clear.

BLIND EYES HEALED

The Lord said to me, "Sophal, are you happy because eighteen people just got saved? Look at the back door. There is a woman there who has been blind for eighteen years. She is sick and very sad. You are to call her out and pray for her, and I will open her eyes."

I had no experience with hearing the audible voice of God and began to doubt what I was hearing. I was afraid to say anything, so I argued with God.

"Lord," I said, "there is no one blind here. We have only young people here."

I had led the people back into worship when the voice came again, and this time it was much more forceful.

"Look," God said, "there is a woman at the back door. She is eighty-one years old. She has been blind for eighteen years. Call her up front, and I will heal her."

God's voice was so loud in my head that it felt like the whole sky was full of His voice. I began to shake, but I still couldn't bring myself to call for the blind woman. I just stood there and cried. Finally, gathering courage, I asked, "Is there anyone here who is blind? God wants to heal you."

Everyone looked at one another, but no one stood up, so I called out, "It is an eighty-one-year-old woman. You have been blind for a long time, but today God is here to heal you."

At that moment the back door of the church opened. The elderly blind woman had been sitting outside because there was no room in the church. A girl led her into the sanctuary. Here was the blind woman the Lord had been talking to me about! I got excited and felt a bit bold, but only for a moment—because as I watched the woman being led to the front, I realized that I had no faith. What was I thinking? Here I was preaching for the very first time and calling for a blind person to be healed!

When the woman got to the front, I asked her, "Do you believe God can heal you today?"

She began to shake and replied, "I have heard my daughter talk about church, but I had no time to come until today. We arrived late, and there was no room inside, so we sat outside. I heard you call twice, but I thought you were talking about someone else until I heard you say God wants to heal an eighty-one-year-old woman. Tomorrow is my birthday, and I will be eighty-one. I know it is me that God wants to heal today."

"How many of you believe God will heal this woman today?" I asked the congregation. The entire place erupted with a roar.

I had no idea how to pray for healing. I knew only what I had read in the Bible. I had seen a lot of our leaders pray for the sick, but I didn't know what to do, so I just pleaded with God to heal her eyes.

"You are a glorious God," I said in my heart. "Everyone wants to see this woman healed. I remember well how You healed me and how You answered my prayers to preach, so please answer my prayers and heal this woman now."

Turning to the woman, I commanded her eyes to open in the name of the Lord Jesus Christ. She was weeping and tried to open her eyes. I placed a book in front of her and asked her if she could see anything, but she could not. I went back to pleading with God for her sight.

"You are the One who told me to call her forward and that You would heal her," I said to God. "But here she stands, and she still can't see. Many are watching to see if You are real."

At that moment the Lord spoke very strongly to me: "Do not doubt My healing. Tell the people to repent."

Because most of those present did not fully understand repentance, I preached on repentance and then began to pray again for the woman's sight to be restored.

At that point the entire congregation was kneeling on the floor, praying with me and weeping.

Suddenly the woman began to shout that she could see. I ran to her, and she proceeded to tell me the color of my shirt and tie. Then, taking the microphone from my hand, she turned to the congregation and exclaimed, "This is the real God! This is the real One!" Jumping up and down she shouted, "Jesus, Jesus, Jesus!" before falling to the floor under the power of His presence.

The service went on for a long time that morning. Nobody wanted to go home. We all just wanted to stay in God's presence. News of her healing spread as she told everyone she could about how God had healed her. Her family was wealthy, and her son-in-law was a doctor, but no amount of money or medicine had been able to cure her blindness.

PLANTING CHURCHES

With a grateful heart, the woman who had been healed invited us to her home for a celebration. Her house was lovely, and the table was set for a feast when we arrived. She had cooked all day just for us. Partway through dinner, she got up and walked over to stand behind me.

"You know my circumstances well," she said. "I was blind for eighteen years and suffered greatly. But now I can see because Jesus Christ has healed me."

Then she invited me to share the gospel with her family. Glory to God: that night her entire family gave their lives to Jesus—more than one hundred of them!

Before the evening was over, this dear woman came to me with a large key. "This is the key to my house," she said. "I am giving it to you because God told me that you needed this house for your church. It now belongs to God."

Because of her generosity we were able to open a church right there in her home. Her entire family attended the first service and became the foundation of that church plant. God had healed her eyes and touched her heart.

Within two years of planting that church, we were able to plant several more around Phnom Penh. The only province we were able to minister in outside the city was the northwestern province of Battambang, and so most of our work was centered in Phnom Penh in the early days. I think I planted at least seven churches in the city in that two-year period, and I hadn't even finished Bible school.

Many began to call me "Pastor" because God Himself had anointed me with that title, but I was not yet comfortable with the title. I wanted things to be in the proper order. I was still in Bible school and personally felt it wasn't right for me to become a pastor until I had finished. There were others who felt strongly that I was already walking in the role of a pastor, and so in 1973 I was ordained, even though I was still in Bible school. I became hungry to pastor a large church and prayed fervently about this, but the Lord did not open that door for me at that particular time. We continued to evangelize in and around Phnom Penh and to plant house churches.

Despite setbacks, the churches I had planted in the city flourished, operating with great strength. Even though we were a young church with a lot of young people who had little or no experience "doing church," God was there in our midst and moving powerfully in miracles, which brought explosive growth. In the forty-seven years that Christian and Missionary Alliance missionaries labored for the gospel in Cambodia, from 1923 to 1970, only five hundred people came to Christ. Then in 1973 the church exploded as a result of the miracles that were taking place.

From 1973 to 1975 thousands of people gave their lives to Christ in Cambodia. Every day hundreds were saved. There were not enough churches to receive the new converts, so we planted house churches everywhere. It was a busy and exciting time. Many of us were still learning what it meant to be a Christian, and although we were babes in Christ, we were able to minister to others thanks to the anointing of the Holy Spirit. Little did we know what was to come.

PART TWO

WAR

CHAPTER 5

I N 1975 THE war spilled into Phnom Penh. The Khmer Rouge were on the verge of capturing the city. The loss of life was staggering. About two weeks before the fall of the city, God spoke through Nared-Nareth, telling us to hold a last-supper fellowship meal at the Bible school. He also told us to send the Burke family back to America.

"Todd, you must go home now," NaredNareth said. "The Lord says for you to take your wife and children and go back home to America. There is an opening now for you to leave."

The Burkes were very reluctant to go, but they eventually agreed because they had come to know that when God spoke through NaredNareth, it was important to listen. They left the country two weeks before the city fell, taking three orphans with them.

WE SAY GOOD-BYE TO THE BURKES

The night before the Burkes left, the church gathered for a meal. At one point NaredNareth stood and said, "I don't know what will happen now that God is telling this man and woman of God to go back home to America. I don't know how much suffering is coming, but we must stand in unity. Stay together. Do not separate. Stay together and pray, and God will bless us."

All of us said our tearful good-byes to the Burkes, and then it was time to get them to the airport. I was the only one who could drive. Bombs were falling all over the city. The airport had become a target and was officially closed. Only cargo planes were allowed to land. Often the bombing was so intense that the cargo planes could not actually touch down. They would simply fly over the runway and drop food. When they were able to touch down, it often was just for a short stop. They soon would take off again. Regular passenger planes were no longer in operation.

Cars were not allowed on the roads. I knew I had to get the Burke family to the airport even if it meant I would be killed in the process. I put the family in the back of my pickup truck and began to make my way through the city. Normally it was a fifteen- to twenty-minute drive to the airport, but that day it took us more than an hour. There were so many butchered bodies on the roads that I had to drive slowly to navigate around them. Many of these people had had their heads, arms, and legs cut off, and body parts were strewn everywhere.

We finally made it to the airport. A cargo plane flew overhead but could not land. Then a second one came by, but it couldn't land either. We didn't know what to do. I found a policeman, and he suggested I drive right out on the runway where the planes were attempting to land. That would give the Burkes a better chance of getting on a plane if one did in fact touch down.

I drove onto one of the runways and parked my truck. After some time another cargo plane flew in, and this one was able to land. Quickly Todd and his family ran to the plane and scrambled aboard. The pilot gunned the engines, and the plane roared off down the runway and was in the air again as quickly as it had landed. We didn't even have time to say our last good-byes. I wept in grief and fear as I drove home, not knowing if we would ever see Todd and his family again, and not knowing what would happen to us now.

THE DIASPORA BEGINS

When the Khmer Rouge captured Phnom Penh, the government fell. Our church family stayed in our building, praying. We remained inside for three days before soldiers came with guns. They were going house to house, telling everyone to leave the city immediately. They banged on our doors with their guns and said, "You and your family—your entire group—must leave. You have three days to leave the city. If you don't go, you will die because the Americans are coming to bomb the city."

When the Khmer Rouge evacuated Phnom Penh, they forced the entire population into the rural countryside, leaving the city a virtual ghost town. We thought we were going to stay because we had not heard the Lord tell us to go, but the solders returned and ordered us to leave.

About six hundred of us left the church together on foot. At first we were able to stay together, but after a few days some of our group became separated. We had a lot of babies with us, many of them orphans. We had a little bit of milk and water with us that we used to feed the babies, but, tragically, within weeks all of them had died. I did not know it, but the Lord was about to separate me from my church family. I was about to enter a time of great suffering and persecution.

We were about halfway to the Thai border when the Lord spoke to me. "Sophal," He said, "you and your family need to go back home."

I couldn't imagine why the Lord was telling me this. It made no sense. To return to my hometown of Takéo meant we would have to backtrack through the outskirts of Phnom Penh. The odds that we would make it alive were slim. I didn't understand what the Lord was doing. Normally when I received a strong word from the Lord that would impact other people as well as me, I would share it with others. But this time I kept it to myself. For two weeks I told no one.

We continued our progress toward the Thai border and eventually reached a mountaintop from which we could see Thailand. The border was close, and everyone was excited.

I went to sleep that night thinking we would be safely in Thailand soon, but the Lord spoke again. "Sophal, you and your family need to return home."

It was a strong word this time, and I knew I had to pay attention. I fell down on top of that mountain, shaking in fear before the Lord. For three days I lay on the mountain, shaking, unable to talk to anyone. Then the elders approached me.

"What has happened to you, Brother Sophal?" they asked.

"I'm sorry, dear brothers and sisters," I said. "Please forgive me. Two weeks ago the Lord spoke to me and asked my family to return home, but I didn't obey Him. I don't want to go home. I want to stay with all of you. I love you. I want to go to the Thai border with you. But He spoke to me again a few nights ago, and His word was very strong this time. He is commanding me to return, and I know I must obey. I cannot go on with you. If any of you want to return with me, you are welcome to come. But whatever you decide, I know I must return."

Takéo and Another Good-Bye

We spent the rest of the day talking and praying about what we should do. The Lord had told us to stay together. But in the end my mother and father, an uncle and nephew, and a few children decided they were to return with me. In all, eleven people would go with me to Takéo.

Tearfully we left our dear brothers and sisters in Christ behind and began the long journey back home. We each had a Bible, and those in our group who continued on to the Thai border each had a Bible as well. We could only trust that the Lord would protect them. Later I would hear of their fate.

After arriving in Takéo, we were able to live in peace for a few weeks. We had daily Bible readings and times of prayer. The Khmer Rouge did not yet have strong control over every aspect of daily life in the city, and we were able to enjoy what would be our last days of freedom for a long time.

Late one night the Lord woke me and said that I was to leave my parents' house immediately. The next morning, during our time of Bible study, I felt that the Lord was confirming His word to me. We read from Genesis 12, in which God called Abram to move from his birthplace, from his father's house, and go to the land the Lord would show him.

Reluctantly I told my parents it was time for us to leave. My father struggled to understand what God was saying. The war was intensifying, and he wanted all of us to stay together. I had to convince him that this really was the Lord's doing, that I needed to leave in order to obey the Lord.

"Father," I said, "even though we may not see each other for a long time, if I am obedient to the Lord, we will see each other again. I feel certain of it. Please don't worry."

My wife and I left that day with our two daughters, Martha and Phally, and two orphans. Not long after our departure, Khmer Rouge authorities came to my father's house looking for me. They told my father that they wanted me to come to work for them. If we had been there, I would have refused to go with them, and they would have killed me because I was a Christian working with the Americans. My simple act of obedience saved my life.

CHAPTER 6

OVER THE NEXT four years, with the communists in power, my family and I were forced into labor camps outside the city. We were tortured and suffered a great deal in the camps. Several times I was marked for execution. Each time, however, the Lord intervened and my life was miraculously spared.

The Khmer Rouge were atheists and forbade us to practice our faith, but we did anyway. We continued to evangelize and bring people to the Lord. I hid my Bible in the ground during the day. At night I would take it out, and a small group of us would read the Word together and sing. One day the guards found my Bible and took it from me. We loved that Bible so much. We were heartbroken and felt like we had no hope. But my wife was a very clever woman, and she hatched a plan to get my Bible back.

"Go to the guards and tell them you need some paper to roll cigarettes," she said. "They know that thin paper is best for rolling. If you ask them for pages from the Bible, they will agree that the thin pages will make excellent cigarette papers."

Seeing the wisdom of her suggestion, I worked up my courage and went to the guards to ask for paper.

"Why do you want paper?" the guard asked.

"My wife and I and our group would like to smoke," I replied.

"I have never seen you smoke before," he said.

"Well, sir, we never did smoke, but we want to start because there are a lot of mosquitoes here, and the smoke will help to keep them away," I answered. "The pages of that Bible I gave you are thin and will make excellent rolling paper."

He agreed and handed me my Bible so that I could tear out some of the pages. Even though he complained, I took most of the New Testament.

HIDING THE WORD IN OUR HEARTS

Ecstatic, I went back to our group with my treasure. We passed the pages around, a page at a time. Each day we would read the page we had been given and then pass it on. In that way we were able to read most of the New Testament on a continuing basis. We were desperate for the Word.

We had nothing to write with or write on, but our memories were good, so we wrote God's words on our minds and in our hearts. In one night many of us could memorize an entire page before passing it on to someone else. Within a couple of months we had memorized what scriptures we had of the New Testament and didn't need the precious pages anymore.

It was too dangerous to be caught with any type of printed material, especially a Bible or pages from a Bible. It was a miracle that I was not executed when the Khmer Rouge confiscated my Bible. Anyone with an education and those who could read and write were prime targets for execution.

The Khmer Rouge divided the prison population into sections. At night we were separated, but during the day we were in groups of about one thousand. We were not allowed to talk about Christianity, so we would whistle Christian songs as we worked as a way of identifying ourselves to other Christians. In a couple of months we were able to identify a lot of brothers and sisters in Christ. Because we had memorized so much of the Bible, we were able to share our faith with less danger of being detected. We added about sixty-five new believers to our group in this way.

The "Buffalo Doctor" Baptizes New Believers

Then one day the Lord told me to baptize the new believers. That seemed like such an impossibility, given our situation. But I had learned that nothing is impossible with God. It was amazing how He took the everyday circumstances of life in the prison camp and used them to enable me to do what He asked of me.

In Cambodia at that time there were no tractors or machinery of any type to plow the fields, so we used water buffalo. I had grown up around buffalo and knew how to work with them. I had seen my dad use bark from certain trees to heal wounds on our buffalo. I knew how to mix the bark with water and apply it to the wounds. The guards would bring me injured buffalo, I would treat their wounds and pray over them, and in a few days they would be healed. In this way I developed a reputation as the "buffalo doctor."

There were always plenty of sick buffalo that needed my care, so the guards assigned three people to help me, and together we built pens to enclose the animals. The mosquitoes were very bad at night, so we would gather wood and build fires to ward off the bugs and help keep the animals warm. During the day we also gathered grass to feed them since many were too injured to walk. As I walked through the buffalo pens, putting grass down for them to eat, I would talk to them.

"Brother," I would say, "please eat this good grass for me, because if you live I also will live. But if you die, I will die too. Eat in the name of Jesus Christ and be healed."

The guards had told me that if even one buffalo died, I would be executed.

We talked to the buffalo and prayed over them, and at night we would sing hymns over them. The guards said we were crazy, but we knew that they would sneak down and hide outside the pens at night just to hear us singing over the animals. They became somewhat fond of me because of the way I cared for the sick buffalo. When I sensed that I had built up enough goodwill to ask for a favor, I worked up my courage and went to the guards with a special request.

Life in our buffalo pens was messy at best, so when it came time to take buffalo back to the Khmer Rouge authorities, the animals were usually quite muddy and dirty. I told the leader of the guards that I felt it was more respectful to return clean buffalo to the authorities, and he agreed with me. I suggested washing them in the river—but because we could have as many as a hundred buffalo in our care at any one time, I requested that the guards would assign more people to help. I told them I needed lots of strong men to work with me.

"I have sixty-five strong men skilled in working with water buffalo available to help me," I said.

These were the sixty-five new converts the Lord had instructed me to baptize.

"Go ahead and use your men," the guard said.

And so, together with the new converts, I took the buffalo to the river, and as we washed them, I would instruct each man to duck quickly under the water. As they went down I would say, "I baptize you in the name of the Father, the Son, and the Holy Ghost." In this way I was able to baptize all sixty-five people. We washed the buffalo, prayed, and sang worship songs, and the guards had no idea what we were doing.

After the war, in the 1990s, some of the Khmer Rouge guards from that time when I tended the buffalo came to me to talk about Jesus. They had seen how the God of the Christians had healed the buffalo and protected me, and they wanted to know more. I was able to lead them to the Lord, and together they started a house church.

I eventually was taken off buffalo duty and assigned to carpentry work, building houses in the surrounding villages. I was a good carpenter. I knew how to cut wood and how to build a house, and these skills served me well. I built quite a few houses in the Pursat Province. After the war, I took visiting missionaries to see the houses, and we were able to plant a house church in the area.

CHAPTER 7

DUE ENTIRELY TO the anointing of God on my life, I often seemed to emerge as the pastor and leader of any group of Christians I was with. I would gather a team around me, much like a church leader would do, except that we had no physical location to call home. It was simply too dangerous even to contemplate such a thing as assembling together.

The local Khmer Rouge authorities took notice of how many people followed me around and became suspicious. They thought I might be a political leader trying to stir up rebellion. One day they approached our group and told us that we would have to leave the area that night. We had to "move," they said. *Move* was their code word for "be killed." They would simply come and take people out of the villages and kill them.

The Killing Fields

We were forced to march throughout the night. For eight hours we walked without rest. We eventually came to a field.

Tractors had dug huge holes in the ground. There were hundreds and hundreds of bodies in the holes.

The Khmer Rouge would line people up along the edge of the pits, and one by one they would beat them with a bamboo rod, knocking them into the holes. They didn't want to waste ammunition to kill people. When they had filled up the holes, they would use the tractors to cover the bodies with dirt. These were what later became known as the "killing fields."

It was about four o'clock in the morning when we arrived at the killing fields. So many people were crying out for help, but there was no one to help them. There were sixty-eight of us in our group, all young believers, because the older people had all died. I didn't want the others to see the killing, so I volunteered to go to the front of the line. I felt I had finished the work the Lord had given me to do, and I was ready to die.

There were only ten people in front of me in line. It is hard to explain what it felt like, standing there waiting to die. There was nothing else to do but cry out to God.

"Lord," I cried, "I don't want these evil people to kill me like this. Take me home, Lord. I want to go home with You. I don't know how to kill myself, and I know that is not Your desire. Please do something, God. I don't want dirty men with dirty hands to kill me. I just want to go home with You."

Suddenly I fell down. At first I thought I might be dying. I just lay there, with ten people in front of me, near the edge of the pit. And then I heard the sound of a horse and the voice of a man. I looked up and saw that a man on horseback had ridden up to the soldier responsible for the killing.

"How many people have you killed tonight?" he asked the soldier.

"Only about a thousand," came the reply.

"Stop!" ordered the solider. "The Vietnamese Army is close to the city. Stop the killing. Let those who are still alive go back where they came from."

For a short time I just lay on the ground, unable to move. God had heard my prayers and saved my life and the lives of all those with me. We had been ready to go home to Him, but that was not His plan.

As we gathered together, I told my dear brothers and sisters: "Don't worry. Keep your faith; don't give up. Just keep walking with the Lord, even when you are facing death."

We remembered the words of Psalm 91:7: "A thousand may fall at your side and ten thousand at your right hand, but it shall not come near you" (MEV).

The guards commanded us to stay at the killing fields until morning, when they would release us to go home. We didn't really have a home to return to—just a small place where we stayed together in groups. We sat throughout the predawn hours, talking among ourselves. Many in our group were afraid and wanted to run away.

"No," I counseled them. "We are not to go anywhere right now. We were told to stay right here, and I believe that is what God wants us to do."

But they wouldn't listen. All but seven of them got up and ran away. A short time later we heard gunshots. The guards killed them all. Out of our group of sixty-eight, only eight survived, and we were alive only because we had been obedient to the voice of God.

SALVATION IN THE MIDST OF WAR

For more than three years we lived under the Khmer Rouge communist rule. My wife and I were thrown in prison and almost killed three times. In the forced labor camps we were fed rice soup. We were given no meat or vegetables, only rice with water. Forced to work for eighteen hours a day, many died of starvation.

Under the Khmer Rouge, families were separated. My wife and I were allowed to see each other only once a year, for three days. How we looked forward to those three days. When we came together we would celebrate communion.

Once, someone gave me three potatoes. It was a miracle. The entire country was forced to live on rice and water, and our family had three potatoes. We saved them in anticipation of our three-day visit, and when we came together we cooked the potatoes and made a bread of sorts for communion. At midnight we celebrated the Lord's Supper. Using our potato bread and wine made from the juice of coconut leaves, we held hands, prayed, and fellowshipped.

While we were sitting there, I heard the sound of a pistol being cocked. I looked up and saw a soldier pointing his gun at me.

"Where did you get the potatoes?" he demanded. "Everyone else has only rice, and you have potatoes."

"God gave me these potatoes," I said.

"I don't believe you," he replied. "I think you stole those potatoes from the government. You are a bad man."

Thinking that I was about to die, I suddenly became very bold.

"Sir, I am a Christian," I said. "I am telling you the truth. I believe in Jesus Christ. I have not lied to you. I didn't steal these potatoes. God sent a man to give me these potatoes because He loves me."

"Tell me the truth," the soldier said, "and I will let you go free. If not, I will kill you."

"Just kill me and let the others go," I replied. "I am the one with the potatoes. But if you will come a bit closer, I will share the story with you first."

Now holding two guns, both trained on me, the soldier moved closer. Gripped by a boldness that only could have come from God, I began to tell this man about Jesus.

"Brother," I said, "do you know how much Jesus loves you? He doesn't care how bad you are or how many people you have killed. Today is your day of salvation. If you will hear the Word of God and repent, you can receive salvation. God is here to set you free."

I was talking fast at that point because I thought I was going to die. I wanted to make sure he heard all the good news before he shot me. "Give me just five minutes, God," I silently pleaded.

"I want to tell you about Jesus Christ," I said. "There have been many times when people have tried to kill me, but each time God has spared my life. I stood on the edge of a pit, with ten people in front of me, waiting for the bamboo stick on my back, but God spared my life. Many hundreds of people have died around me, but God has spared my life. I am here to tell you that Jesus is God, the real God. Today I beg you, listen to the Word of God. Repent! Stop killing people. God loves you, brother. Jesus loves you!"

I saw the guns begin to shake in his hands, and then he fell to the ground. The power of the name of Jesus came on this man and overcame the evil that gripped him.

"Tell me more stories," he said. "I have never heard about Jesus. Up until now whenever I point my gun at someone, I just kill them. I don't hesitate. But you speak with such power that I am afraid."

"That's because God is with me, brother," I replied. "Now you must repent and give your life to the Lord. Jesus loves you. Jesus will set you free."

"What must I do?" he asked.

"Sit down here, and I will pray for you," I said.

With that, he motioned to the other soldiers behind him to drop their machine guns and sit down with him. Looking at this group of broken men, I said, "Father, forgive them. Save them, Lord. These men were evil, but now they are willing to change. Save them, Father. Use them."

After a time of prayer the soldiers prepared to leave. They offered to bring us more food and promised not to tell anyone else what had happened. We were released to return to our respective labor camps rather than being shot for stealing food. God had saved us again. The power of His mighty name is stronger than any other power in heaven or on earth.

CHAPTER 8

As the war drew to a close, the fighting became fierce. The Khmer Rouge were driven back to the border by the Vietnamese-backed army. In a last, desperate attempt to hold off the Vietnamese long enough to escape across the border, the Khmer Rouge created a barrier of land mines around themselves and put us Cambodians along the front line of the minefield so that the Vietnamese would have to kill us first. About four or five thousand of us were gathered there, enclosed in this minefield with the Khmer soldiers.

Vietnamese soldiers in tanks approached the minefield, stopped, and set up a big speaker. "Is there anyone among you who can speak Vietnamese? Come forward," they said. "We cannot speak Khmer, so we need a translator."

I knew how to speak Vietnamese. When I was growing up, there were many Vietnamese in our village. Sometimes the children would pick on me, so my grandfather had urged me to become friends with them and learn their language. I did and became quite fluent.

"I speak Vietnamese," I said as I stepped forward.

They handed me the loudspeaker and ordered me to translate.

"No more Khmer Rouge," I said. "All the Khmer Rouge are gone. Everyone can go back to your homes now. Go back to your homes with peace and joy; no more war."

Then I continued: "Today, my brothers and sisters, is a blessed day. God has set you free so you can return home. No more Khmer Rouge. Jesus has set you free! Hallelujah!"

"What did you just tell them?" the Vietnamese commander asked me.

"I was just thanking the Vietnamese for coming to rescue us," I replied.

Silently, however, I prayed, "Forgive me for lying, Lord. We have so little time left. We have to preach to the people all the time, Father. You provided a loudspeaker, so I felt it was time to start telling them about Jesus."

The commander then said to me, "Ask your people how many of them want to leave now for their hometown."

"How many of you want to give your lives to Jesus Christ right now?" I asked. Then I preached to them about Jesus. Many gave their lives to Him that day as I led them in the sinner's prayer. I think about five thousand people got saved that day.

Leaving us in order to pursue the Khmer Rouge, the Vietnamese put me in charge of the Cambodians, telling me to lead them back to Phnom Penh. The journey back was glorious. We had to walk slowly, and whenever we stopped, I would climb into a tree and preach to the people. We would sing songs as we walked, and joy would come upon the crowd. When we arrived in Pursat, about 174 kilometers northwest of Phnom Penh, God instructed me to stay there for a few weeks. During that time I was able to begin training leaders for the church.

RETURN TO PHNOM PENH

As we approached Phnom Penh, we were told that only Vietnamese were permitted in the city itself. I was allowed back in to translate, and on January 18, 1979, I set foot once again in the capital. It was nighttime, and I found a place to curl up until daylight and then headed for our church.

Several years before, at our last supper with Todd and DeAnn Burke and their family, NaredNareth had told us that whoever returned to the city was to write his or her name on the back wall of the church. Remembering her words, I went to the back wall and read two names there, MuranMaran and Ngorn Som. Of the six hundred people who had left the church when the city fell, only two had returned so far. I added my name to the wall.

"Sophal Ung, January 18, 1979," I wrote.

It was four weeks before anyone else returned to the church.

MuranMaran and Ngorn Som had escaped with their families to the Thai border, but out of the approximately seventy people with them, they were the only two survivors. Each had seen all their extended families killed, and MuranMaran had lost his wife and children as well. I had lost a brother, my sister, a daughter, my uncle, and other extended family. The three of us just sat and prayed.

MuranMaran was one of the leaders in our church in Phnom Penh before the war. Ngorn Som was with the large group from our church that continued on to the Thai border after I turned back and went to my hometown in obedience to God's instruction. That had been in 1975, when the Khmer Rouge were about to take Phnom Penh. Ngorn Som had been an orphan, just a young boy then.

Each person in the large group that had continued on to the border had carried a Bible with them, and because of that they all had died on the killing fields—all except Ngorn Som. He had been beaten with bamboo rods and had fallen among the bodies in one of the pits, but he had not died. The Khmer Rouge had not bothered to bulldoze dirt over them. He had been able to climb out of the pit and, eventually, make it to the Vietnamese border, where he had stayed.

THE CHURCH GROWS AGAIN

To our delight we discovered that the Bibles that were stored in the church during the war had been left undisturbed. There had been a great deal of looting in the city, but apparently no one had considered the Bibles worth taking. Several thousand of them were still in the church. They had been left behind by a group of missionaries from England who had fled the country at the start of the war. We also had hymnals in English, Cambodian, and Vietnamese.

The church had been largely untouched by looting. We discovered that a fisherman's net had been stolen from the wall in the library. It was part of a scene someone had painted on the wall of a man throwing a net to catch fish. But it didn't matter that the net was gone because God's Spirit was still in the church.

With our building intact, Bibles and hymnals in hand, and the strong presence of the Holy Spirit in our midst, we felt it was time to open the doors to our church once again. We decided to approach the government's minister of religion and ask permission to preach the gospel. We were granted an audience with him, and sitting in his office, I said to him, "We are Christians, and we want permission to worship God. This country has Catholics, Buddhists, and Muslims who have permission to worship. As Christians, we ask for permission also."

"How many of you are there?" he inquired.

"We have only three families," I replied.

"With so few, why don't you just go to the Buddhists?" he asked.

"We believe in Jesus Christ, not Buddha," I replied. "Will you help us?"

I pleaded with him. Every morning I would be at his office, pleading our case. I think he grew tired of me and finally stamped the necessary paperwork. With official permission in hand, we began to hold services in our building. Within a few months about 150 people were part of the church.

Our little congregation was a brokenhearted group. Every person there had lost so many loved ones. As we gathered together in prayer and worship, God came into our midst and began to heal shattered hearts and minds. Within a short time our church was full again. But our joy was short-lived. The Vietnamese would not allow gatherings of more than four people.

They ordered us to close the church, and we complied—or so they thought. Undeterred, we became an underground church. We met in small groups all over the city, every day. The only time we were allowed to hold large gatherings was for a wedding or to celebrate the birth of a baby, and we took advantage of those times.

The government thought they could stop the spread of Christianity by restricting our meetings, but what we were not allowed to do in the natural, God did in the power of His Spirit. He moved upon the whole country of Cambodia, and hundreds of people were saved and healed.

CHAPTER 9

B ECAUSE THE COMMUNISTS had tried to kill anyone with an education—anyone who could read or write—precious few educated people were left alive in the country after the war was over. Muran-Maran was one of them. His experience and expertise in banking attracted the attention of the new government leaders, and they quickly placed him in a position of authority, as head of the banking system. Ngorn Som became a teacher.

The Vietnamese-occupied government began the arduous task of rebuilding the infrastructure of Cambodia. My ability as a translator was very valuable to them. I was assigned to train people to step into leadership positions in government, education, finance, and many other institutions. In my training meetings I would translate for a few hours and then I would teach about Jesus.

I was quickly promoted to the position of mayor of Phnom Penh, over security and protection. With the three of us in positions of authority, we did not waste opportunities to build the church. Although we had the government's permission to hold church services and preach the gospel, the authorities began to look for ways to shut us down.

Our meetings were restricted to one hour a week even though Buddhists and Muslims were allowed to worship twenty-four hours a day, seven days a week. The government began to spy on us and followed us wherever we went.

CAPTURED BY THE VIETNAMESE COMMUNISTS

One night, having just dropped off MuranMaran at his house, I was making my way home through the darkened streets on my motorcycle when the authorities stopped me. Pretending to be motorists in need of assistance, they asked for petrol. As I transferred some of my gasoline to their vehicle, I looked up to see two guns pointed at me. About twenty men with machine guns surrounded me. They blindfolded me, tied my hands, chained me like an animal, and threw me in the back of an old, black Mercedes-Benz van. I recognized it as belonging to the Ministry of Interior (the secret police).

After driving for what seemed like a very long time, we arrived at the jail. I was thrown into a small, unlit cell. For three days, chained hand and foot and blindfolded, I lay there.

"Lord," I cried out. "You have called me. I have opened a church and preached the gospel everywhere possible. What have I done to deserve this? Why am I being treated this way, Lord?"

After three days they unchained me, took me to a room, gave me a cup of hot tea, and began to question me. "Who do you work for?" they asked.

"What do you mean?" I said.

"You are meeting every day. You are traveling from group to group, and there are many groups. You must be working against our government. You are a political enemy. Do you work for the CIA?"

"No, I am not CIA," I replied.

"Do you work for King Sihanouk?" they asked. King Sihanouk was living in exile in China after being ousted by a military coup in 1970. For a time he had aligned himself with the Khmer Rouge.

"No, I don't work for King Sihanouk," I replied. "All I have is a Bible. I preach the Word of God. I even have a permit from the minister of religion."

No matter what I said, they would not believe me.

"If you answer truthfully, we will let you go home," they said. "Your wife and children are waiting for you at home. If you don't tell the truth, we will put you in jail."

"I cannot answer you any differently than I already have," I told them.

DAYS OF SUFFERING

They continued to question me, asking the same questions over and over, and I kept giving them the same answers, but they would not believe me. They seemed to think I was a Christian from America working for the CIA.

At one point the officer in charge became angry. He was a big man. He came up to me and hit me so hard I fell off my chair. He then began to beat me without mercy. I started to bleed from my ears and eyes and nose. This went on for what seemed like hours. Periodically they would throw water on me to revive me so that he could beat me some more. I lost consciousness after a while.

When I would lose consciousness, they would take me back to my cell until I was awake again and then bring me back to the interrogation room and beat me again. When they realized that the beatings would not make me talk, they stopped beating me and just left me in my cell. For three days I lay there, bloody and bruised. My face was horribly swollen.

"God," I cried. "What is happening? Please help me! They have almost killed me many times, but You have always set me free. I have been obedient to everything You have asked of me, and here I am in jail. What is happening? Help me, Lord!"

I talked to God all day and all night for three days, but He did not respond. He remained silent.

After three days they brought me back to the interrogation room, and the beatings began all over again. On the second day they pulled the fingernails from two of my fingers. It was indescribably painful and bloody, and they did nothing to bandage my fingers. They asked the same questions over and over, and I told them again and again that I was just a preacher, teaching people how to go to heaven. I tried to tell them that I was not in any way subversive to the Vietnamese government in Cambodia, but they would not believe me.

Frustrated, they then began to shock me with electricity. They made me lie on the floor. My whole body shook with each jolt of electricity. It was unbelievably cruel and painful. I lost consciousness.

When I awoke in my cell, my whole body was swollen from the electric-shock torture. My cell was pitch black, and my hands and feet were chained. They would unchain one hand at night, but still it was almost impossible to move. This was how I lived each day. The prisoners in the jail were treated worse than dogs.

They fed us only one small bowl of rice soup a day, in the dark. We had to eat like animals because our hands were chained. They would set the bowls in front of us, and if we didn't empty them within twenty or thirty minutes, they would take the bowls away. Everyone was hungry, and many died of starvation within a short time of arriving at the prison. The communists liked to torture people, and they were masters at it. I got to the point where I couldn't handle it anymore.

"Lord," I cried in anguish. "This is too much suffering. I just want to go home to be with You. Please let me go home." But God was silent.

They tortured me in this manner for six months. When they finally realized that I was not going to give them any new information, they gave up. They stopped beating me and moved me to a slightly better cell. Slowly I began to heal.

SINGING IN THE DARK

Every night I could hear the other prisoners crying in pain. Many would die during the night, and in the morning I could hear the doors opening and the bodies being taken out. We prisoners could not see each other, and we were never allowed to congregate. The cells were very small and not high enough for standing up. All we could do was sit in the darkness. The only way we could communicate was to talk through the holes in the wall that connected our chains.

One day I was crying out to God in despair. "Lord, where are You?" I wept. "I am so alone."

Then suddenly I remembered the story from the New Testament of Paul and Silas in prison and how they began to sing. The two of them had been a team, and as they prayed and worshipped God, He sent an angel to open the doors of the prison and set them free. Although my hands and feet were chained, my mouth was not, and so I decided I would sing.

It wasn't easy to sing in that filthy prison cell. I was starving and in great pain, but I sang the best that I could. I began with one of the songs the children in our church used to sing in the morning. It was called "I've Got a River of Life Flowing Out of Me." As I sang, the peace of God came on me. During all those months of torture I had found no peace, but as I sang to the Lord, He refreshed me and gave me peace and joy. I continued to sing, day and night, the same song over and over.

One night the man in the cell to my right spoke up and said, "Hey, brother, why are you so happy? Did they give you food? Have they unchained you? Are you free?"

"That's a great question," I replied. "And I have a great answer for you. Let me tell you why I am happy. Because I have God, and His name is Jesus Christ. I am a Christian. Even though my hands and feet are bound, my mouth is unfettered. That is why I am singing to God."

This man was fifty-five years old and a two-star general. He had been thrown into prison for the rest of his life. He wanted to know more about Christianity. As we talked, I told him the story of Paul and Silas in prison and how God had sent an angel to open the doors.

"If your God opens the door for you and you get out, will you go and tell my wife that I am here?" he asked. I told him I would surely try.

When the communists caught someone and put them in prison, they told no one. They were very secretive.

When someone disappeared, no one knew for sure where they went. The communists would try to catch people along the roads early in the morning or late at night when no one else was around, like they did with me. People would disappear, and families would never know what happened, though most suspected that their loved one had been captured by the Vietnamese and sent to prison or killed. No one dared ask, though.

This general wanted to sing with me, and so we sang. Pretty soon the man on the other side of the general heard us singing. I was able to lead him to the Lord, and he joined his voice with ours in song. I think that there were about four hundred men in that area of the underground prison. Little by little we were able to spread the gospel and pass along the song. Many men gave their lives to Jesus. Hour after hour, day after day, and into the night we would sing the words to "There's a River of Life." It was a song for us all, for the verses of the song gave us hope in our situation.

A HARD BUT PRECIOUS MISSION

Many continued to die from starvation and disease, but those of us still alive kept on singing. Peace filled my heart, and I knew why God had kept me in that filthy prison. He wanted to reach all of those dear ones with the message of the gospel before they died. I know that hundreds of people were saved in that prison.

It was a hard mission God had given me. When I hear people say they want to go and preach the gospel, and they say, "Take me, Lord—I will go anywhere," I don't think most of them know what they are really saying to God. When I ask people where they want God to send them, I often hear them list beautiful places such as Hawaii. They want to preach the gospel in beautiful surroundings, not in filthy prisons.

If God had asked me beforehand if I wanted to preach the gospel in prison, I would have said, "No, Lord. There is too much suffering in prison. Send me somewhere else."

But God didn't ask me. He never told me He was going to send me to an underground prison, but I thank Him a million times over that He used me in that way because so many were saved before they died.

As the months went by and I languished in that prison, I became so very tired. So many people died. I lost the friends I had made. The prison became quiet because there were no people left to sing with me.

"Lord," I said one day. "I have finished my job here. Please let me go home now. I have two beautiful daughters and a lovely wife waiting for me. I miss my family, and I miss my church. Many people are waiting for me, Lord. Please send me home now. I can't stay here any longer. I can't sing anymore. I am so tired. Please just let me go home to my family, Lord."

A few days after this prayer I fell down and could not get up. I know exactly what happens when people die, and I was very close to death. But I wasn't afraid. I had lost my fear of death.

"Take me home, Lord! Take me home," I whispered.

CHAPTER 10

I don't know how long I lay on the floor of my cell, but when I opened my eyes I saw a light come into my room. It was the glory of God. The light was made up of many beautiful colors, all shining right there in that filthy, black prison cell. It reminded me of the glory cloud I saw when I awoke from the coma years before.

Then I began to hear people singing. I heard what sounded like thousands of voices singing the words to "There's a River of Life." They were singing in Khmer. It was as if the whole sky was filled with that song, with a thousand voices singing my song.

I opened my eyes again and saw angels surrounding me. They were so close I could reach out and touch them, but I couldn't move. There must have been thousands of angels. The ceiling above me was filled with them. Each angel was extraordinary looking. Years later in Bangkok, in 1991, I would have this same physical visitation from the Lord. The angels just kept singing my song over me. I began to sing with them, and I felt like I was flying among them. Our singing released an incredible joy in that place.

I don't know how long this visitation lasted. To my recollection it seemed that I was in the glory of God for several days. The angels eventually disappeared, but the glory of God remained with me. It was such a beautiful experience that it is hard to put it into words.

Then God spoke to me very strongly.

"Sophal," He said. "Fear not, my son. I have set you free. It's time to go home now. But there are two things you need to obey: You are not to talk and not to eat anything until I tell you. Your eyes will see Me when I return, but it's not time for you to die yet."

"I hear You, Lord," I said. It was many years after I got out of prison before God allowed me to share what had happened to me during His visitation.

After the Lord spoke to me, the light left my cell, and I found myself in darkness and silence again. My hands and feet were still chained. Then two beautiful female nurses came into my cell with food. It smelled so good. I could smell it even before they got to my cell. They put plates of many different kinds of food in front of me, unchained me, and told me to eat.

"Once you are strong enough, you will be allowed to go home," they said.

I got so excited at the sight of that food. I was so hungry. But God had given me strict instructions not to eat and not to talk to anyone. Here was all this good food in front of me, and I couldn't eat any of it. And I couldn't talk to these nice nurses to ask them to tell my family that I was alive and coming home soon.

This continued for three days, and then the warden and one of the guards came to my cell with a key. "What happened here?" they asked the nurses. "Why hasn't he eaten the food? Is he dead?"

"He is almost dead," they replied.

"Check him," the guard said. So the nurses checked my pitiful body.

"This man is evil," the warden said. "He is a leader for the CIA. He doesn't want to die in this prison. Have him taken out and thrown in the river."

SET FREE: GOD'S PROMISE FULFILLED

They unchained me, but I was too weak to walk, so they carried me outside and threw me in the back of a truck. It was close to sunset. The truck smelled bad, and ants began to crawl all over my body. I was nothing but skin and bones. I smelled horrid, and my hair and nails were long and filthy. I was in a lot of pain from the effects of starvation. I knew that my internal organs would be shutting down soon.

"Take me home right now, please, Lord," I cried.

Finally two men came out and got in the truck. We drove away, and it seemed like we drove around for a long time. I could tell we were near the river. I could hear them talking about throwing me into the river.

"Please, Lord, don't let them throw me into the river," I pleaded. "You know I cannot swim and that I am very weak. If they throw me in the river, I will surely die. You told me You were setting me free. You promised, Lord. Keep Your promises to me, please, Lord."

One of the men stopped to buy some alcohol, and they proceeded to drive around all night, getting drunker and drunker. I heard one of them say, "This man looks like he is a good person. Maybe we could take him somewhere and drop him off."

"Do it, Lord. Speak to him, Lord!" I pleaded. "Speak to these bad men and change their lives, Lord. Change their minds. Let them take me somewhere safe."

They both were drunk and lost, but they managed to find a hospital. They drove over to some banana trees that were behind the hospital and dropped me under the trees. I lay there all night, too weak to move. Early the next morning some cleaning women who were walking by heard my cries for help and had me taken into the hospital. I was put in a room, bathed and cleaned, and hooked up to an IV. I was too weak to speak. It was several days before I was strong enough to talk with the doctors.

ESCAPE BY NIGHT

One day a Cuban doctor came into my room accompanied by government officials. He told me they had received a report that I was a Khmer Rouge leader.

This accusation angered me greatly, but because God had told me not to talk, I did not respond. The doctor returned a few days later with a young boy who translated for him.

"Sir, what is your name?" the doctor asked. "Why did they catch you and put you in prison? Why did they bring you here? Tell me because I want to help you."

God opened my mouth, and I was able to tell him the whole story. "My name is Sophal," I began. "I am a Christian. They put me in jail because I was preaching the gospel. They accused me of seditious activities. They said I was engaging in political activities; that I was a CIA agent."

As I spoke, the doctor began to cry.

"Brother, I too am a Christian," he said. "I believe God left me here to help you. I was supposed to go back to Cuba two months ago, but for some reason I was told to stay another two months. No one here knows I am a Christian. We are two brothers in Christ in a communist country. How can I help you?"

"Can you help me get out of here as quickly as possible?" I asked.

"No," he replied. "There are security forces guarding you and guarding the entrances and exits to the hospital."

We prayed, and then he assured me he would get word to my wife and family of my whereabouts and my condition. He helped me dictate a short letter, which he then gave to the cleaning woman, one of the women who found me under the trees. She delivered the letter to my wife and later became a member of our church. My wife was granted permission to visit and brought clean clothes.

With my strength somewhat restored, I was anxious to leave the hospital as quickly as possible. I knew the authorities would eventually return and take me back to prison. Together the doctor and I hatched a plan. He said he would leave the back door of the hospital unlocked for me but that I would have to get out by myself. He wouldn't be able to help me. And I would have to do it immediately because he had received word they were coming for me the next day.

I was too weak to walk on my own. "Lord," I cried out, "You need to help me get out of here. I can't walk." I knew my church was praying for me.

The tension of waiting until dark was exhausting. At about seven o'clock in the evening, a storm rolled in. The wind began to blow hard, making a lot of noise in the coconut trees outside. As the lightning flashed and the thunder crashed around the hospital, it started to rain. It was a torrential downpour that went on for hours. The storm knocked out electricity throughout the city. I knew it was time for me to get out of there.

Thanks be to God, He sent the cleaning woman to help me! She was tiny, but she picked me up and carried me out of my room and to the back wall of the corridor near the back door. A flash of lightning revealed two guards not far from us. We saw them, but they didn't see us. She quickly dropped me against the wall and fled. Crying out for God's help, I began to crawl toward the door. It took me a while to reach the door because I was so weak. I tried to open the doors but couldn't.

"Blind their eyes, Lord. Don't let them see me!" I cried silently.

And with that, I crawled under one of the chairs there by the doors. With each lightning flash I could see the guards and their machine guns. I kept crying out to God, and somehow the door opened. I don't know if the cleaning woman came back and opened it for me or if an angel opened the door for me, but it opened, and I managed to get outside.

It was raining hard, and in my weakened condition I began to shiver. Barbed wire fencing surrounded the hospital. There was a gate in the fencing, but it wouldn't open, so I just tried to climb through the wire on the gate. The painful barbs tore into my skin. Suddenly a beautiful hand opened the gate and then held it open for me and helped me walk through and down the road. A car was waiting with the Cuban doctor at the wheel.

I knew I couldn't return home. That would be the first place the authorities would look. So I had the doctor drive me to the house of a friend, a policeman. His wife greeted me at the door with a hug. They hid me in the basement, fed me soup, and cared for me, but we all knew I wouldn't be able to stay with them very long because the authorities were looking for me. They would throw anyone who helped me into jail. I was still very sick and weak.

When the authorities discovered I had escaped from the hospital, they immediately went to my house, arrested my wife, and began to interrogate her.

"You are the ones who put my husband in jail," she told them. "You have told me nothing of his whereabouts. How could I have helped him escape?"

Her boldness saved her. They let her return home, but from then on our house was watched. My policeman friend heard that they now were going house to house looking for me. I had a big price on my head. They said I was a Cambodian leader of the CIA and a Christian working with the Americans.

CHAPTER 11

A T THAT TIME every section of the city had a communist leader in charge who watched all the houses in his section very carefully. My friends said I must leave right away, but I had nowhere to go.

I was able to get word to my wife, Kim-Ean, and she came up with a plan. Our friend Ngorn Som agreed to help. He was the young man who as a child had survived the killing fields and eventually returned to Phnom Penh after the war to write his name on the wall of our church. He came in the dark of night on his small Vespa motorbike, bringing women's clothes, and a group of women proceeded to transform me from a wretched-looking man into a beautiful woman.

Hunted

My hair was still quite long, and I weighed only about fifty-five pounds. They put makeup on my face, fixed my hair, and got me into a dress. Then they gave me a purse and taught me how to walk like a woman. Ngorn Som was to be my husband.

On a Saturday night we left together on the Vespa and headed into the city to attend a party. As a government official, Ngorn Som had been invited, and he was allowed to bring his wife. When a man brought his wife to official functions, security checked only the man, not the woman. I was to be silent and act the dutiful wife.

We wound our way through the city on the little bike, successfully navigating several checkpoints, thanks to the mercy of God. We had just crossed a bridge and gone through a checkpoint unnoticed when I spotted the black Mercedes van ahead of us. I knew immediately that it was the one belonging to the Ministry of Interior that had taken me to the prison.

Quickly we detoured down to the river, hid the bike, and jumped into the water. The van passed by twice, looking for us. We stayed in the water, shivering with cold and fear until we felt sure it was safe, and then we fled.

Over the course of the next day I was able to make my way to my sister-in-law's house, and there I stayed for two months. I did exercises to strengthen my legs, and with their help I was able to regain some strength and walk again. Then we received word that the communists were in the vicinity going house to house looking for me. I knew it was too dangerous for me and my family to stay, so I began to plan my escape.

I decided the river might be safer than the road. Fashioning a raft out of trees and bamboo, I waited until dark and then set off, traveling about nine miles, until the sun came up. The cold water sapped my strength, and when I finally made it to shore I collapsed and could go no farther. I felt like I was going to die.

Following their early-morning custom of ritual cleaning, people from the nearby villages came down to the river to wash, and found me. A compassionate man took me back to his house, wrapped me in warm blankets, set me in front of a wood fire, and cared for me. Within a few days I was strong enough to think about traveling again. I wanted to get to the coastal province of Kompong Som (now called Sihanoukville) via Takéo, my hometown.

I got word to my wife and told her it was time for our family to leave Cambodia. We had no option but to go to the Thai border. We could not risk staying in Cambodia any longer. She agreed, and we made arrangements. I was able to find a truck big enough to carry my family, and together we drove until we were close to the border. Leaving the truck behind, we continued on foot. We walked for three weeks, only at night. Minefields were everywhere. One wrong step would bring death. We prayed constantly.

AN ANGEL IN THE NIGHT

After three weeks of picking our way through the mines in the dark of night, my wife could go no farther. She was pregnant and ready to deliver the baby. We were in the jungle alone. I had no idea how to help deliver a baby. "Can you wait until we get to the Thai border?" I asked her. It was a crazy question, but that was what I was thinking.

But, of course, babies do not wait. My wife lay down in the dirt of the jungle, and I began to pray fervently. With her cries ringing in my ears, I called out, "Lord, I don't have any experience with this. Please send someone to help us! I need help right now!"

And then a miracle happened. I felt a hand on my shoulder and turned to see a woman standing behind me. "Can I help you, sir?" she asked. "I am a midwife."

We were in the middle of the jungle in the black of night, and God sent a midwife! She quickly took charge, telling me to find wood, build a fire, and boil some water. As I went out looking for wood, the wind began to blow and it started to rain. I didn't know how I was going to build a fire with wet wood.

When I got back to where my wife and the midwife were, I was greeted with another miracle. It was raining all around us, but where we were was perfectly dry. Not a drop of rain fell on us. The midwife shooed me off to look for wood again, and when I returned, there was my wife, sitting up beneath a tree holding our son. As she cleaned the baby she sang over him.

I was overjoyed with the whole situation. I had been hoping for a son because we had two daughters. Here we were, having suffered so much as a family, and the Lord had given us another miracle and the blessing of a son.

After spending time with Kim-Ean, I asked, "Where is the midwife? I want to thank her."

"I don't know," was Kim-Ean's reply.

I searched, calling for the midwife, but didn't find her. I believe she was an angel sent by God to deliver our baby.

We huddled together throughout the night. It rained all around us, but the area we were in stayed dry. Kim-Ean was exhausted and didn't have enough milk when the baby was born, but our new little son was quiet throughout the night. The next morning he began to cry like a healthy newborn, and Kim-Ean was able to nurse him. We rested in that place in the jungle for a few days and then resumed our trek.

Another Miracle

I made a sling for the baby with a scarf, and—with the baby in the sling on one side and my wife holding my other hand—we walked slowly, resting frequently. We walked in this manner for two weeks, until we ran out of water. It was hot, and we all were thirsty. We could go no farther without water. We knew we would die unless we found water soon, so we began to pray.

Sitting in the shade, I remembered the words of Psalm 121, which tells us to lift our eyes unto the hills.

"My help comes from the LORD, the Maker of heaven and earth" (Ps. 121:2). We claimed that word for our situation.

"Lord, You know how much we need water," we prayed. "You know our every need. Thank You for taking care of us on this journey—for all the things You have done. Now we need Your living water to sustain us, or we will die. I know You promised me I would not die until You returned, so I thank You for the water You are going to provide."

While we were praying, my wife and baby fell asleep. As I continued to talk with God, an old man walked by us without slowing down. A few minutes later he came back and said, "Oh, I see you have a baby. Do you need some water?"

"Yes, we desperately need water," I replied.

He had a canteen of water with him and we took it all. About that time Kim-Ean woke up, but she was unable to thank the old man because he had disappeared, just like the midwife had! We were overcome with joy at yet another miracle from God for our little family.

With water to drink, we were refreshed enough to resume our journey. It was extremely slow going. Kim-Ean was still quite weak. Minefields were all around us. We could see the bodies of those who had died. It was not safe to walk during the day. The Khmer Rouge and Thai robbers were everywhere. All we could do was pick our way through the jungle at night. Within a few weeks we were quite close to the border, heading toward the refugee camp of Nong Chan.

BANDITS

We were no longer alone now. All around us were crowds of refugees trying to get to the border camps. One night as we were making our way along in the midst of the crowd, we were stopped by a band of robbers with guns.

"Are you heading for the border? Do you have money?" they demanded. "We want your gold and your money, or you will end up like them," the leader said, nodding toward a tree with a pile of bodies under it. Most were dead but some were still alive. We could see them moving.

I reached over to cover Kim-Ean's eyes. I didn't want her to see any more horror and suffering. She was so weak.

"Lord," I prayed, "these men are for real. They will kill us if we don't give them money. Help us!"

Then I remembered the twenty dollars in my pocket, given to my wife to take with her to the hospital with my clothes. Someone at the church had given it to us. It was all we had.

"Sir," I said, "I tell you the truth. I have no gold or money, only twenty dollars. Here it is. Please let us go free."

He refused the twenty dollars. "You look like rich people," he said. "Why don't you have money with you? If I check you and find out you are lying, I will kill you."

Boldness in the Lord came over me. "Sir, I am a Christian," I said. "I would not lie to you. Twenty dollars is all I have. Here, take it and let us go. I am here to tell you that many months ago the communists put me in jail. I prayed to God and He helped me escape. Then a few weeks ago we were alone in the jungle when my wife started to have her baby, and God sent a midwife. Then we found ourselves without water, and God sent water.

"Please believe me. We only have twenty dollars. We have suffered so much already. Please take the money and let us go. I am a man of God. Today I am speaking the word of God to you. Repent."

"What are you talking about?" he asked.

"I am a Christian," I replied. "I believe in Jesus Christ. I see the people you have killed. This is a sin. You must stop killing people now. Today is your day of salvation. You can be set free right now. Stop robbing and killing. Please let us go. We are just trying to get out of this communist country to find a place to live in freedom."

We talked for quite a while, and then the baby began to cry. "Oh, you have a baby," he said. "I want the baby. If you don't have money, I will take the baby. Give me the baby."

"Lord," I prayed, "don't let this man with dirty hands touch my baby!"

He tried to take the baby from us again and again, but my wife wouldn't let go. Finally I said to him, "We don't have anything. Just kill us all together. We are willing to die now together. This is too much for us."

Something came over the man at that moment. Looking at us, he said, "OK, you look like good people. You are different from the others."

Putting a hand on my shoulder, he turned to the two women working with him and told them to give me the money, gold, and diamonds they were holding. They had been collecting valuables from the dead bodies. They handed us the money, and he told us to take it and leave with our baby.

My initial reaction was to refuse the money. I didn't want their dirty money. I thought they were just playing with me—that they were going to give us the money, let us walk a little way, and then shoot us.

"Sophal, listen," Kim-Ean said. "Only God can bring things from evil hands into the kingdom. Jesus was given a bad name, and they crucified Him; but after the Resurrection the name of Jesus has been lifted high. We have been obedient to God, and He has provided this money for us. Take it now."

So we took the money and walked away from the robbers with our baby in our arms, all the way to the refugee camp on the border.

When we arrived at the camp, we joined the thousands already there waiting in line for food and supplies from the United Nations. Each week they would give out food, clothes, blankets, and medicine. Thousands of people came to receive whatever they could. The distributions were made on Sunday, so if you arrived on a Monday, you had to wait the entire week to get anything. Nobody had much of anything, and many died from starvation and disease.

PART THREE

THE CAMPS

CHAPTER 12

OUR FIRST NIGHT in the Nong Chan refugee camp I asked if there was any way to get food. I was told there were vendors about two miles from the camp. With money in hand from the robbers, I asked around to see if anyone wanted to go with me to the vendors. Lots of young people volunteered. I took about twenty with me and we headed toward the vendors. I was able to buy a lot of rice, noodles, and all kinds of other food.

Together with the young people, we carried it all back to the camp and fed as many people as we could. Everyone kept asking me how I was able to get food, and I told them God had supplied us. When we had finished eating, I shared the gospel with them. Then I told them the story of our journey and the miraculous ways in which God had cared for us. Everyone was weeping, especially the old people. Their hearts were so touched by our story that they wanted to stay with us.

Every day I would preach to the people, even when we were standing in line waiting for food and supplies. And I continued to make the trip to the vendors to bring back food and feed as many as possible.

MINISTERING TO THE REFUGEES

One day I suggested we build a large house and all live there together. About one hundred young men volunteered to climb the mountain and cut wood and bamboo for the house. I paid them a dollar a day for their labors. Within a month we had constructed a house big enough for everyone in our group. We all moved in and began to hold services there every day. It was our first house church in the refugee camps.

About three hundred people came to the first service, which was about the number we had been feeding weekly. The United Nations continued to supply us with food. Many people who had been thinking they would take the supplies given to them and return home to Cambodia decided instead to stay right there in our house church. Life was better there than in Cambodia under the communists.

With a wife and a new baby, I really needed separate living quarters. I sent the young men out again to cut wood and bamboo, again paying them a dollar a day. They built a house for my family and were able to build houses for others as well. I estimated that each house cost me about thirty dollars. We built three hundred to four hundred houses. We were able to help people because Jesus had given us the provision.

So many people had been healed and saved. I felt it was time to baptize everyone, but there was no river nearby. After talking with the Thai soldiers, I agreed to pay them one hundred dollars to transport us all in a big truck to the river, which was about an hour away. We spent the whole day at the river, baptizing people, then celebrated with communion.

The last person we baptized was slain in the Spirit while he was under the water. He went out, and after we had taken him out of the water, we were not able to wake him for several hours. It was almost as if he were dead. When he finally woke up, he told us his name was Seng and that he was a leper. He said that when he went under the water, it felt so hot that he couldn't move. He was completely healed of any trace of leprosy and began speaking in tongues.

There was another man named SamedSameth who was also healed of leprosy that day after his baptism. Both men eventually emigrated to America.

Seng came under the ministry of Ché Ahn, who today is the pastor of HRock Church in Pasadena, California, and ministered in the United States and Cambodia in the late 1990s and early 2000s. Seng was one of my disciples before he went to America. I married him to a beautiful young woman, and they opened a doughnut shop and planted a church in Modesto, California, before coming under Ché Ahn's ministry. SamedSameth is now a pastor in Long Beach, California.

Many years later when I was preaching at a large pastors' conference in Long Beach, both Seng and SamedSameth came forward when I asked if anyone had a testimony to share. I didn't recognize them until they shared how God had healed them of leprosy in the camps after the war.

Youth With A Mission (YWAM) and a number of other Christian organizations began relief work in the camps. Between my house-church ministry and the efforts of those Christian organizations, virtually every Cambodian who passed through that camp was exposed to the gospel.

KHAO-I-DANG CAMP

I stayed in the camps for three years, from 1980 to 1983, because I felt God wanted me there to preach the gospel. The church grew quickly, and within a year we had about one hundred twenty house churches scattered throughout the camps.

Every Sunday we would gather together for worship. There was no building big enough to hold us all, so we would meet outdoors. I estimated we had about six thousand people gathering each Sunday in Khao-I-Dang Camp for worship. When I preached, I would climb up into a tree. YWAM gave me a small generator and a sound system. Using a ladder, I would climb a tree and preach to the crowds gathered below.

There were about fifty thousand refugees in the Khao-I-Dang Camp during the three years I lived there. The camp was divided into sections, with a few thousand people in each section. Each section had a leader. I planted four or five house churches in each section. It was a powerful time of ministry for me. I was free to preach the gospel daily. Spread between all the house churches, we were holding up to ten services a day in the camps.

One day a young man came to the service. He had been born crippled. At age seventeen he was so ashamed of his inability to walk that he wanted to kill himself. His parents were with him that day, and we prayed. Both his parents got saved.

This family lived in Section 19 of the camp. After we prayed, I told them I felt I was to come to their house for dinner, and they graciously extended an invitation. Not long after that a blind man came to me with a word of knowledge he had received in a dream. He told me I was to go to Section 19 to minister. I felt certain this was confirmation that I was to minister to the young crippled man.

When I arrived at their home, dinner was prepared, and a worship leader was waiting to lead us in worship before we ate. I felt led to go to the boy's room before dinner, and there I found the young man. His mother was with me, and as she introduced us, she began to weep.

"Today is my son's eighteenth birthday, and he is so ashamed of his condition that he planned to commit suicide last week," she said.

My heart was so touched by this wonderful young man that I stopped things right there.

"Dinner can wait," I said.

We brought the worship leader to the boy's room and began to sing and praise God. I looked at the young man, and he was smiling. With his permission, I laid hands on him and asked God to heal him. As I prayed for him, it was clear to me that God had orchestrated my visit to the house that day.

"I command you to walk in the name of Jesus," I said to the young man.

Shaking, he stood up and began to walk, taking only a few steps before falling down. This young man, crippled from birth, had just walked! We continued to pray because I believed that God intended to heal him completely. He got up and walked again and again. When it was time for dinner, he joined us.

I wasn't able to visit this family again for about a week because things were busy in the camp. Late on a Saturday afternoon I headed for Section 19. When I arrived at the house, it was quiet. No one was at home. Then I looked up and saw the young man coming toward the house, carrying water from the well. Just the week before he had been able to take only a few steps without falling down, and now here he was, strong enough to carry water from the well. He was very excited to see me and to show me how well he could walk.

The next day he walked the one kilometer to church and gave his testimony. As word of his healing spread, newspapers and magazines from Bangkok sent reporters to interview him. The reporters would come to me and ask, "What happened? Tell us what happened."

"All I know is that God healed him," I would reply. "He is old enough to speak for himself. Why don't you ask him?"

He visited every house church in the camp, sharing his testimony. Today he is a pastor in America.

OUR FAMILY REUNITED

I was very happy living and ministering in the camps. I felt like it was where God wanted me, and I had no desire to leave. God had opened doors for me, and now I was free to preach and plant churches, something that had been impossible under communist rule in Cambodia. My only heartache was that our two beautiful little daughters were still in Cambodia living with my mother. We were not able to bring them with us because we had fled for our lives from the communist authorities who wanted to kill me.

After much prayer we felt like the Lord wanted us together again as a family. The problem was that I couldn't return to Cambodia because I was an escaped prisoner. Kim-Ean said she would go back for the girls. It was a journey of faith for her. She traversed through the jungle back to our hometown, carrying the baby the whole way. Our son was only three months old at the time. It was a very difficult journey.

When she got to our hometown, she found my parents' house empty. She spent about a month at the church praying over the situation, not knowing what else to do. In addition to our two daughters we had adopted three orphans to bring back. Kim-Ean passed away in 1985, and the details of her trip are fuzzy in my mind now, but she managed to find the children and bring them back to the camp. Somehow God enabled her to make the long journey with an infant and five small children.

When word came to me that Kim-Ean and the children were in the jungle close to Nong Chan Camp, I went to find them. No one could travel during the day—only at night, to avoid detection by the robbers and the Thai soldiers. The night I found Kim-Ean and the children, it was cold and raining hard. We had no shelter and were afraid to stop, so we pressed on throughout the night. It was terribly difficult, and I was not sure the little ones were going to make it.

We came to a large river and had to cross it to get to the camp. None of the children could swim. We prayed, and then I left the children on the riverbank and took Kim-Ean and the baby across. Then I tried to bring two of the children at a time, but one almost drowned, and we had to go back. Slowly and carefully I swam across with each child. The children all were crying. We suffered so much.

It took quite a while to get across and back with each child. The last two who were left alone on the far side were very frightened there in the dark and wanted me to take all of them across at the same time, but I said no. It seemed like it took forever, but I managed to get my whole family safely across the river. It was almost dawn, and as we set off again, along came a gang of robbers. They had weapons and spoke Khmer.

"Give us everything you have," they demanded. "All your money, everything."

We were cold and wet and exhausted, and this was almost more than we could bear. My wife didn't say a word. We were all huddled on the ground. I could see that the children were terrified, so to calm them I said, "Don't be afraid. This man is your uncle. He came to receive us into the camp."

To my surprise he said, "Yeah, I am your relative. Don't be afraid, children. Stand up!"

They took everything we had except the clothes on our backs. We were exhausted, hungry, cold, and frightened. For a while we huddled together and prayed, and when we felt strong enough we set off again. We traveled by night for two days, without food, before we reached the camp.

As we got closer, there were others around us, running toward the camp. One young woman was carrying a baby, and she began to follow us.

"Where do you want to go?" I asked.

"I am alone with the baby," she said. "My husband was murdered. I just want to get to the camp."

It was still dark and almost impossible to see anything. "Help us to find the way, Lord," I prayed.

We just kept walking, and suddenly I saw a small light in front of us. There was no noise, no voice, only the small light moving slowly in front of us. As we walked, the light moved ahead of us. We followed it throughout the night until we got very close to the camp.

By that time the camp had been closed to any more refugees. It was surrounded by double barbed-wire fencing and guards armed with machine guns who would not hesitate to kill anyone who came near. They didn't ask questions. They would just shoot to kill. The fact that we were able to get into the camp without being shot was another miracle.

When we got within about one hundred meters of the outer fence, a man appeared and told us to go through the gate. He even showed us where to go. I felt certain at the time that it was a real man who stood there in front of us, but as soon as he showed us where to go, he disappeared. It was dark and difficult to see clearly, but I remember thinking that he looked like what I pictured Moses looking like. Having this man show us an open gate in the fence was like Moses parting the Red Sea. It was a miracle.

As the soldiers heard us approaching the camp, they began to shoot. Everyone hit the ground. The babies began to cry. Whenever they heard a noise, the soldiers would shoot again. Mothers with babies pinched the noses of their infants and covered their mouths to keep the children from crying.

We could see the sentry towers and the guards with machine guns and the two layers of fencing. My son was so excited to finally reach the camp that he ran through the second gate and up to the third gate before the soldiers began to shoot. I heard the gunfire and was certain they had killed him. I didn't know that he had fallen into a hole and was unharmed.

The other kids ran into the bushes, leaving me, Kim-Ean with our baby, and the other woman with her baby standing out in the open. There was nothing we could do. We just stood there as the soldiers approached us.

"Brother," I said, "we have escaped from the communists in Cambodia. We came here for protection. We have nothing. We are just looking for a place of freedom. We want to serve the Lord here. It is just me and my family."

"You can come in," he said. "If you pay us five hundred dollars each, we will let you go free."

We called the children out of the bushes. We still didn't know that our son was alive, in the hole. We thought he was dead.

"We don't have any money," I replied.

At that moment our son appeared out of the dark. He had managed to climb out of the hole but was so scared he was shaking like a leaf. We forgot all about the soldiers and the money and just began to jump for joy. It was a miracle reunion.

The soldiers motioned for us to go through the gate, and we walked into the camp. They didn't say another word to us about the bribe that night. But just to be safe, we managed to collect the money and gave it to the Thai soldiers the next morning. Finally our family was together and safe.

CHAPTER 13

THE YOUNG WIDOW with the baby made it into the camp with us, but tragically her baby had died when she pinched his nose and covered his mouth to keep him from crying. She was so grief-stricken that she didn't want to live anymore. She had lost her husband and now her baby.

Our first day back in the camp we gathered around this young grieving mother and her dead baby, and I began to intercede. "Lord, she has only one baby," I prayed. "She doesn't want to live without her baby. I need Your help now, God! Let the life come back into her baby, now!"

I prayed like that for what seemed like twenty or thirty minutes, pleading with God for the life of her baby. She was holding her dead child and crying the whole time when, suddenly, the baby coughed and came back to life! It was an unbelievable miracle. The child had been dead for more than twenty-four hours.

Overjoyed, I held the baby and thanked the Lord for giving this child's life back. As the infant began to cry, I handed him back to his mother, and we all stood there weeping over what God had so graciously done. The Thai soldiers saw everything that had happened.

Together with this woman and her child, our whole family went to church that day to give witness to what God had done. This young mother stood with her baby and gave her testimony in front of several hundred people, telling them how God had raised her child from the dead. Her testimony turned the whole church upside down.

THE COST OF THE GOSPEL

There were many orphaned children in the camps, and many babies and young children with their families. With the influx of foreign-aid workers, many of these children were able to receive much-needed care. One of the workers was a lovely woman named Hannah from an organization called Christian Outreach, who worked in the feeding programs. She approached me one day and said, "Sophal, I want to help with your little boy and the baby who was raised from the dead. I have several nurses who can help with this work. I will send one to you."

For many months this nurse lived in our house in the camp, caring for the babies, as well as for my entire family. Thanks to her loving care, we all were stronger and healthier within a few months.

Our physical health was being restored, but our two daughters, Martha and Phally, carried heavy emotional scars. Months went by, and neither of them would talk. The severe trauma they had experienced had overwhelmed them. They were unable to process all that they had seen during the Khmer Rouge occupation, my time in jail, and the brutal trip through the jungles to the Thai border. They had lost their childhood.

Martha was largely silent until the age of sixteen. She was only eight or nine years old when all of this happened. Phally would talk a little, but she too remained silent most of the time. They saw many miracles during our time in the camps, but they carried a great deal of anger over what had happened to us and to those around us. God has healed them, and today they can talk about their ordeal, but their healing took many years.

There is a price to be paid for the gospel, but God is always there to help us. He doesn't always send what we need straight from heaven. Sometimes He works through the people around us, sometimes He sends His angels, and sometimes there are those wonderful times when He Himself comes in a personal visitation to talk with us and give direction. I cannot help weeping whenever I share my story because so much of the goodness of God is evident in every day of my life.

When Kim-Ean returned with the children, I was still living in Nong Chan Camp, right on the border. We opened a house church there called Nong Chan

Church. Nong Chan Camp was smaller than Khao-I-Dang Camp, and they were about a two-day journey apart. After Kim-Ean and the children returned safely, I moved my family back to Khao-I-Dang Camp.

Bibles!

Many relief organizations came to the border camps to help the refugees—organizations such as YWAM, World Relief, and World Vision. They were not allowed into Cambodia, but they were permitted to work in the camps. They provided doctors and nurses and set up day-care centers. Their workers would arrive in the morning and return to the nearby city of Aranyaprathet in the evening.

I worked with these organizations and developed good relationships with their volunteers. When they would ask me what we needed, I would always tell them, "Bibles!" I asked for thousands of Bibles. There was one man in particular, with World Relief—I think he was from Canada—who would bring Bibles to the camp every day. His son, who spoke fluent Cambodian, would come with him.

Thanks to his efforts and the efforts of many others, we managed to accumulate a good supply of Bibles and were able to store them in one of our churches. On food-distribution days, when thousands of people would be lined up, we would hand out the Bibles with the food. I continually would give away all our Bibles and ask for more. People walked away from those long lines happy, with food and Bibles in their hands. We had all kinds of Bibles to give away: picture-book Bibles, reference Bibles, the Gospels. We had other kinds of Christian literature too. We gave it all away.

Since no aid organizations were allowed in Cambodia, God got Bibles into the country via the refugees who came to the camps for food and supplies. They would return home with their food—and their new Bibles. I believe one of the reasons God kept me in the camps for so long was to get those Bibles into Cambodia.

Life in the camps was better than it had been in Cambodia. The Thai government accepted us, and the United Nations worked with Thailand to stabilize the refugee situation. Each refugee who was granted permission to remain in the camps was issued an identification card. We would use our cards to receive food and supplies. It was wonderful to be taken care of and to be free to preach the gospel. This freedom enabled our house churches to grow and prosper spiritually.

Despite all these improvements life was not easy in the camps. A great deal of evil was present. The other Christians and I constantly cast out demons, cared for the sick, and ministered to those in need. It was an intense time of learning for me. God trained me well, and in turn I trained others. I would bring in leaders, teach them for a few months, and then send them back to their own churches. There was no time for formal seminary training. Yet all of those we trained have matured and continue to minister today.

Sophal and his wife, Kim-Ean, stand inside their home at the Khao-I-Dang refugee camp in eastern Thailand in the early 1980s. With them are their children (from left) Pheakdey, Phally, Makara, Martha, Okedei, and John. The family had only recently been reunited after Kim-Ean returned from a dangerous journey back into Cambodia to get five of the couple's children. They had stayed behind with their grandmother when Sophal and Kim-Ean fled for their lives from the communist authorities in Phnom Penh. Because Sophal was wanted in Cambodia for preaching the gospel and would have been executed if caught, he could not accompany his wife on her courageous mission. A few years after this photograph was taken, Kim-Ean died at age thirty-nine on September 20, 1985.

PHOTO CREDIT: Photo courtesy of James B. Hearn Jr.

Sophal (center) and Kim-Ean, with their children (kneeling), stand alongside other Christian leaders in front of Sophal's house at the Khao-I-Dang refugee camp.

PHOTO CREDIT: Photo courtesy of James B. Hearn Jr.

Sophal (far right) with the leaders he led to Jesus and trained while planting a church in one of the refugee camps in Thailand in the early 1980s.

These and tens of thousands of other Khmer children, most of them orphans of war, filled Khao-I-Dang and other refugee camps dotting the Cambodia-Thailand border after 1979. The Khmer Rouge controlled Cambodia from 1975 to 1979 and carried out widespread genocide, killing as many as two million people. After a three-year war against the Khmer Rouge, Vietnamese communists gained control of Cambodia in 1979, killing anyone deemed a threat to their fledgling government. It was a time of great upheaval, and hundreds of thousands of Cambodians fled to Thailand for safety.

PHOTO CREDIT: Photo courtesy of James B. Hearn Jr.

The main gate at Khao-I-Dang refugee camp as it looked when Sophal and his family lived there. Some fifty thousand refugees were in the camp from 1980 to 1983—the three-year period when Sophal lived in the camps, preaching, ministering, and raising up Christian leaders.

PHOTO CREDIT: Photo courtesy of James B. Hearn Jr.

Upon entering the Khao-I-Dang refugee camp, Khmer children would swarm to sell hand-drawn note cards of tranquil scenes depicting Cambodian village life. Packets of cards were sold for the equivalent of about twenty-five cents a batch. Legally these were considered black-market sales, as the Khmer people were not allowed to have any Thai baht (money), but the Thai military guards willingly looked the other way.

PHOTO CREDIT: Photo courtesy of James B. Hearn Jr.

Hundreds of bamboo and thatched-roof huts fill the expansive Khao-I-Dang Holding Center for Cambodian refugees in eastern Thailand, five miles from the border with Cambodia. The sprawling compound, which lay beneath a picturesque hill surrounded by rice paddies, was completely enclosed with barbed-wire fencing. Thai military guards armed with machine guns patrolled the perimeters and at night shot at even a noise if one was heard in the darkness outside the fences. Khao-I-Dang opened in 1979 after the fall of Pol Pot's Khmer Rouge government in Cambodia. The last refugees left the camp in 1993.*

PHOTO CREDIT: Photo courtesy of James B. Hearn Jr.*

---

* Photographer James B. "Jay" Hearn Jr. was a member of a YWAM (Youth With A Mission) team in Thailand during the time Sophal and his family were living in Khao-I-Dang refugee camp. Jay began attending a weekly Bible study led by Sophal in his home in the camp. After leaving Thailand, Jay lost touch with Sophal. In 2015 Jay happened to meet author Susan Thompson at a Randy Clark conference in Pennsylvania, and when he heard of the book project, he was delighted to share some of his photographs and memories of his time with Sophal.

Sophal preaches to the estimated one hundred thousand people attending the Phnom Penh evangelistic crusade in 1994. Assisted by his leadership team, Sophal trained five thousand Christian leaders eighteen hours a day for a week to minister to the thousands of Buddhist attendees who were expected to come. The crusade marked the first nationwide assembly of Christian leaders in Cambodia since 1975, the year the Khmer Rouge seized power and outlawed Christianity. An estimated ten thousand people were saved the first night, but police closed down the crusade after only a few days when suicide bombers, strapped with explosives and believed to be aligned with the vanquished Khmer Rouge, were apprehended inside the stadium.

Sophal remarried in 1992. Here, he and his new bride, Deborah, are all smiles on their wedding day. They were married in California at the Vineyard Church of Anaheim and since then have been used powerfully as a team to bring the light of the gospel to those still caught in darkness in Cambodia and elsewhere.

Clockwise from left: Deborah, Sophal, Pheakdey,
and Sophal and Deborah's son, Daniel

Sophal and Deborah (far left) attend the wedding of Sophal's
daughter Okedei to her husband, Vutyhy. Included around the
table are some of Sophal's children who, as youngsters, endured the
horrendous physical and emotional trauma of their family's long
flight from the murderous Indochina regimes of the 1980s.

Sophal Ung, apostle, evangelist, and pastor, today

PART FOUR

AMERICA

CHAPTER 14

Around the end of 1983 the United Nations and the Immigration and Naturalization Service (INS) came to our house in the camp with paperwork. They told us that a bus would be coming for us the next day to take our whole family to Bangkok. We were being repatriated along with twenty thousand other Khmers. The children were excited about leaving, but Kim-Ean was not. We had no family in Bangkok, and one day's notice was not nearly enough; but we were given no choice.

We were transported to Con Buri Camp, a refugee-processing center in the Philippines, where we remained for six months. They screened us for tuberculosis, put us through an ESL class, and instructed us in American culture. At one point we were moved from Con Buri Camp to Bataan, a large refugee camp about six hours from Manila. We were able to plant a church in Bataan during our time there.

One night a strong earthquake hit the area. I had stayed overnight at the church, leaving Kim-Ean and the children in our small house. When the quake hit, Kim-Ean was downstairs and the children were upstairs. She was thrown to the floor by the force of the quake and severely injured. She began hemorrhaging. Doctors were unable to stop the bleeding. Emergency arrangements were made to fly our entire family to America as quickly as possible.

The flight from Thailand to America was extremely difficult for all of us. Kim-Ean, accompanied by two doctors, was made to lie down on several seats that had been rearranged to accommodate her. I tried to care for our six children single-handedly. They all were throwing up, and so was I. It was our first flight, and we did not handle it well. All of this was compounded by the fact that none of us spoke English well. Kim-Ean continued to hemorrhage throughout the flight, with the two doctors working to stanch the flow of blood as best as they could.

SADNESS FOR OUR FAMILY

We landed in Dallas, Texas, and Kim-Ean was taken immediately to Parkland Memorial Hospital. Arrangements were made for our family to stay in someone's garage. Americans were not used to taking in large families such as ours, and although we were grateful to have a roof over our heads, living in a garage with six children was far from ideal.

Each day we took a bus from East Dallas across the city to Parkland Hospital. A transfer was involved, and often we had to wait an hour or more in the heat. I got lost more often than I like to admit, and it was not unusual for the police to help us find our way home.

Kim-Ean was diagnosed with uterine cancer. Her doctors wanted to operate immediately, but I refused to sign the necessary paperwork.

"God will heal her," I said. "No knife is going to cut my wife!"

They continued to pressure me to sign, saying that if she died I could go to jail for refusing her treatment. I prayed and consulted with many people and finally realized that I needed to obey the doctors. The Bible tells us that we are to obey the law, and the law was becoming clear to me; so I signed the forms, and Kim-Ean had the surgery. She recovered and was eventually able to return home.

While she was hospitalized, I had cooked and cared for the children by myself. Only our eldest daughter was old enough to go to school. The rest of the children were home with me all day. Kim-Ean was not used to American food and had great difficulty eating the hospital food, so I would cook Cambodian food for her and take it to the hospital. It wasn't easy getting the food and all the kids on and off the buses. The food would be cold by the time we arrived, but Kim-Ean ate it anyway.

KIM-EAN

Although Kim-Ean recovered from the surgery, she never regained her health. She died three years later, at age thirty-nine, on September 20, 1985. So many had prayed for her healing for months. Corporately, in the Dallas area, Christ for the Nations Institute, Shady Grove Church (now Gateway Church Grand Prairie Campus), and Church on the Rock prayed; additionally our good friends came daily to pray with her.

In the final weeks of Kim-Ean's life a dear friend named David opened his home to our family. He knew we needed a much larger place to live, a place where Kim-Ean could have peace and quiet.

Before she died, Kim-Ean asked for all of her children to be brought to her bedside, including the baby. She narrated her story as we sat beside her, and we wrote it all down. She wanted to be sure that the account of her life was accurate. When she finished her narration, she gave a special gift to each daughter.

Then she turned to me and said, "Sophal, don't forget the grace of God by which we have lived. We have seen so many miracles. Don't forget God and don't forget to teach the children how to follow God. Remember that even in the midst of suffering, even in life and death, don't give up. Even though America is very different from Cambodia, be bold to preach the gospel. I hear the Lord clearly, calling you to continue to minister as you have always done. Don't be sad when I'm gone. Be joyful and serve the Lord with great joy for the rest of your life. Our story must continue."

Our family spent the last day of her life gathered around her bed. About one o'clock in the morning, exhausted, all of us went to lie down except one daughter who remained by her mother's side, holding her hand.

"Please don't go, Mother. Don't leave us," she said aloud. "If you die, I want to go home to the Lord with you."

At about one thirty in the morning, Kim-Ean went home to Jesus, her beloved Savior. Her passing was very hard on all of us. We had been through so much. We were in a strange country with no family around us, and we felt very alone. The house we were staying in had five bedrooms, but in our grief we all moved into one bedroom. We just needed to be together.

Our oldest daughter began to question God. She couldn't understand why God, who had healed so many people, did not heal her mother. "I don't think God loves us anymore," she said.

"I wish I had a good answer for you, but I don't," I replied. "All I know is that when I put my hand to the plow, I don't look back, only straight ahead. I believe God is always good, even when it seems hard to understand His ways. Perhaps someday soon God will answer your questions."

In my heart I cried out, "Forgive us for our unbelief, Father!"

Later God did speak to my heart, telling me Kim-Ean's time on earth had come to an end and that it was her time to go home to be with the Lord. This knowledge brought comfort to my heart, but the children were not able to understand until years later. Brokenhearted and angry, our dear daughter drifted away from the Lord for a time. She was just a child and couldn't understand why her mother had died. We grieved together as a family, and the Lord slowly healed our hearts. Today she is married to a mighty man of God, and together they minister in their local church.

CHAPTER 15

WHEN OUR STRENGTH returned we began holding worship services in our house, and many people started coming. At the same time we started to hold services in a park in the city of Dallas. Every Sunday several hundred refugees gathered to worship in the park. We taught the Word and preached and even had Sunday school classes for the children. One Sunday a police officer approached our service.

"Why are you conducting church services in the park?" he asked.

"Sir," I replied, "we need your help. We are refugees. We worship in this park because we have no building to worship in."

He returned the next week with several other officers to make sure we were OK. The following Sunday, news reporters from two television stations in Dallas showed up at our service with cameras. One of the police officers, a Cambodian, had told them about us. They were very interested and wanted to film a news segment about our service. We made the five o'clock evening news and the Monday evening news the following day.

We didn't have a television, so the Cambodian police officer brought one to our house and we were able to see ourselves on TV. I couldn't understand English at the time, so I didn't know what they were saying, but the whole thing was amazing.

Pastor Olen Griffin from Shady Grove Church in Dallas saw the news segment and began to weep as he watched. Tom Thompson, on the leadership team at the church, felt strongly that Shady Grove should contact me. With Reverend Griffin's permission, Tom showed up at my house the next day, escorted there by our new friend, the Cambodian policeman. Tom didn't know where we lived so he had contacted the Dallas Police Department to find out.

Tom explained how the Lord was touching hearts at Shady Grove Church and invited me to come meet with Pastor Griffin. We jumped in Tom's little sports car right then and headed to Pastor Griffin's house. Seated around a large table in his dining room, we began to talk.

"Sophal," Pastor Griffin said, "we love you. We have a big facility here, and we want to make the building available to you, if you're interested. If not, we'll send a team to help you find suitable space right where you live."

"I'm very interested," I replied. "It only makes sense to use your existing facility. Thank you."

Shady Grove Church began to send two large buses to our area every Sunday to pick up our congregation and bring them to their church. We would have two services on Sundays, one a combined Cambodian/American service and the other a Khmer-speaking service. They gave us a very large room for our Khmer service, and in no time Shady Grove Church became our Cambodian church home. Twenty families from Shady Grove volunteered to help us.

THE EAST DALLAS CHURCH

Our Khmer church grew rapidly, but the Lord began to speak to my heart to plant a church in East Dallas too, which had the largest concentration of Cambodian refugees in the city. There were probably about seven thousand Cambodian families living in East Dallas at the time. With Pastor Griffin's help we found a suitable building in the area and were able to open our church plant.

Shady Grove was a very mission-oriented church, supporting sixty-four missionaries in countries all over the world. Our Cambodian church became number sixty-five. With their support, my monthly welfare income of twelve hundred dollars a month was now supplemented by sixteen hundred dollars a month from Shady Grove. The church sent two families to help me with the new plant in East Dallas, and within a year our congregation had swelled to nine hundred people.

Several other churches in the area came together to help with our new plant. It was a very multicultural effort, with Spanish, Laotian, Cambodian, American, and Hmong all coming alongside us.

As we grew, I felt the Lord telling me it was time to hold a crusade in order to bring everyone together and do some teaching. My plan was to have two tents, one for the services and the other for food and fellowship. Shady Grove Church, Church on the Rock, and Christ for the Nations provided the necessary support. They donated a big sound system, musicians, video equipment, a generator, and all sorts of other things that we needed. The crusade lasted for two weeks.

I preached every night in Khmer, which was then translated into English, Spanish, Hmong, and Laotian. During the day we would take teams into the neighborhoods to knock on doors, invite people to the crusade, and talk to them about Jesus. East Dallas had a very rough section with lots of bars. We took our teams into the bars, and God began to do a good work in the hearts and minds of many lost and broken souls. Many people came to the Lord as a result of our neighborhood evangelism. I pastored the church in East Dallas for about two and a half years, and we were able to plant six more churches during that time.

Christian Broadcasting Network (CBN) and *The 700 Club* heard about what God was doing through us and came with their news and broadcast teams. Someone at one of the churches loaned us a big house, and together with the team from CBN, who stayed with us, we went all over the city so they could see how we fed the poor and cared for children. I worked there in East Dallas just as I had in the refugee camps in Thailand, caring for those in need. I had been given so much since coming to America, and I wanted to give back to the community.

As word spread, people flocked to our church for assistance. Church on the Rock would send us five hundred bags of food a week, including meat, chicken, rice, bread, and milk. The doors of our "store" were open every morning to the poor, and they would line up outside waiting for the food and clothing we gave out. Most of the people who came for assistance were black. Within a short time we were able to develop good relationships with the black, Spanish, Hmong, and Laotian populations in the East Dallas area.

Gradually we noticed a shift happening. Many of the poor were moving from Texas to California because welfare benefits in California were much greater than in Texas. Within four years of starting our church, we lost about half the congregation. They left Dallas to relocate in Long Beach, California, which eventually would have the highest Cambodian population in America.

CHAPTER 16

I WAS THE ONLY pastor in our church in East Dallas. I had no one to help me in leadership— but not for lack of trying. It just seemed that no one would step forward. I preached, led worship, taught Sunday school, and even drove the bus to pick up people around the city.

Finally one day I announced to the congregation that starting tomorrow we were going to fast and pray for a week for new leadership to come forward. I told them that those who felt led to fast and pray would have to stay at the church the entire week. Initially forty people agreed to fast and pray with me. By the third day we had dwindled to twenty people, and by day five we were down to seven people. I was determined to be grateful for those seven.

One of the seven was a young man named Nara, who had been with me for several years in America. He carried a strong anointing. When God spoke, this young man heard Him clearly. Some people said they had seen angels around him.

On the last day of the fast I preached about a miracle of God to those seven people. We all were tired. We had preached and prayed and eaten nothing for six days. We all just wanted to go to bed. We crawled into our bunk beds and quickly fell asleep. I was on the bottom bunk, and Nara was on the bunk above me. Around midnight he began to shake my bed.

"Sophal, Pastor Sophal!" he cried out.

"What is it?" I replied.

"I am hearing the voice of God," he said. "He is saying, 'Tell Sophal to go to Wichita, Kansas.'"

"It's midnight. I'm too tired to go anywhere tonight. This will have to wait until tomorrow," I replied, and I promptly fell back asleep.

A few minutes later the bed began to shake again. He was hearing the voice again and it was telling him that I was to go to Wichita, Kansas—right now. Knowing it must be the Lord, and having developed a healthy fear of God, I got up and began waking others up and asking who wanted to go with me.

OBEDIENCE

I had no car at the time, so I asked if anyone had a car or knew of someone with a car they would loan us. One of the young men had just bought a car two days before and was willing to loan it to us for the trip. He volunteered to go with me. I wasn't a very good driver, and he knew it; I think that's why he volunteered. My nephew said he would go too.

So now I had two people to go with me, a car, but no money for gas. We pooled our change and came up with twenty-two dollars, but we didn't know if it would be enough to get us to Wichita. Nara, on inspiration from the Holy Spirit, called the telephone operator, and we were able to find out how far it was from Dallas to Wichita. We did the math and figured we might have just enough money. It would be close.

I decided "close" was good enough, so we started gathering things to take with us. Someone had thought to put the guitar in the car for worship. We stopped at a 7-Eleven for gas, and as we stopped at the pump, a man pulled up behind us and began beeping his horn. It turned out to be a man who knew of me.

"Where are you going at midnight, Pastor Sophal?" he asked.

"To Wichita, Kansas," I replied. And then I explained the reason for our trip.

"Today is my first day on a new job," he said. "I just finished cleaning a church, and they gave me two hundred dollars. I want to bless you. Take it, please."

Not wanting to take all his money, I gratefully accepted one hundred dollars from him. With more than enough money in hand, we got back on the road and headed to Wichita.

I slept in the back of the car all the way to Oklahoma City and beyond, and then it was my turn to drive. I hadn't been behind the wheel for long when we saw a big sign that read "Welcome to Wichita, Kansas." We had made it!

I was so excited that I failed to notice I was speeding until I saw the police car behind me, trying to pull me over. He told me I had been going almost 80 mph in a 65 mph zone.

Explaining the reason for our visit, which was basically that God had told me to go to Wichita, I asked if he knew of an Asian community in the city—anyone from Cambodia, Vietnam, or Thailand? He directed us to a Cambodian refugee community about two miles down the road. He waved us off with a heartfelt good-bye and no ticket. God had done it again—He had sent a police officer to give me directions, not a ticket!

SOULS FOR THE KINGDOM

We found the Asian community without too much difficulty, but we didn't know who to talk to, so we just drove around for a while, praying and asking God for direction. Then I saw a house with the number 7 on it and a handsome man sitting out front. We stopped the car, got out, and asked him if we were in the Cambodian community.

"Pastor Sophal!" he said excitedly.

About four or five years prior this man had been living in one of the refugee camps along the Thai border.

He had come to our church and eventually went on to lead his own house church. His name was Sok.

He immediately invited us into his house. He had prepared a big meal for his children, but they were late coming home, so he invited us to eat with him. It was another miraculous provision of God. We had fasted for a week, not eaten anything, and driven for hours from Dallas. We were hungry, and God led us to the door of a friend with a table full of food.

As we ate, he told us there were about 750 families in the area and that he had a heart to bring them to Christ but didn't know how to begin. We suggested going door-to-door with him, and after a few hours of rest we set out, knocking on doors and telling people about Jesus. Many people gave their lives to the Lord that day, and we felt like it would be a good thing to baptize the new believers. Someone loaned us a vehicle, and we picked up our new converts and took them to the river and baptized them.

Feeling like our work in Wichita was done, we began to make plans to head home to Dallas when we realized that we had no money. The money we had started out with was long gone. My companions were a bit worried, but I knew God would provide in His own way and His own time.

I stopped by Sok's house to thank him for his hospitality. I prayed prayers of blessing over him and his family, and as we shook hands, I felt something in my hand. It was one hundred dollars. God had provided again!

PROPHETIC ENCOUNTER

Our first stop on the way out of town was for gas at a 7-Eleven. The boys went inside to find something to eat. As I stood there at the gas pump, I noticed a nice park behind the 7-Eleven. A group of about ten people sat on the grass. A young man stood up and began preaching. It was anointed preaching. I went over to the group and just stood there, listening.

"Repent—Jesus is coming back soon! Jesus is coming back soon. Repent!" he said.

"Oh, how I could use a young preacher like this," I thought.

When he finished preaching, we began to talk. When I told him I had come from Dallas, he said, "Do you know Sophal in Dallas?" I couldn't believe it; God was doing it again.

This young man, named Lon, was new to the faith. He had been in Bible school for just five months, and he and his wife had been crying out to the Lord for someone to help him, to mentor him in ministry. He knew he was young and inexperienced, but he had a passion to share the gospel message with people.

In a dream just the night before God had shown him a man whom He was sending from Dallas to help him, and this man's name was Sophal. And then it all made sense: this was why God had sent me to Wichita. And now I understood who Lon was. Sometime before this trip to Wichita, God had told me to find a man named Lon. I had tried but hadn't found him—until now. I found Lon, and Lon found me.

New Leaders, New Church

I stayed in Wichita for three weeks to train Lon and several other leaders. Seventeen families came to the training, and from that group we were able to plant a church, which grew quickly. We decided to hold a crusade at Lon's new church. I returned from Dallas and preached for three days and three nights, and God moved powerfully.

One woman, the mother of a pastor from another church, was healed of cancer. In and out of the hospital and near death, she had heard God speak to her in a dream and tell her that an Asian man would come and pray for her, and she would be healed. Many people gave their lives to Christ during the crusade, and many were healed.

My simple act of obedience—to get out of bed at midnight and agree with God to go to Wichita, Kansas, even when I had no car, no money, and no idea what God was up to—resulted in a new church being planted and many souls being won for the kingdom. God is so good, and His mercies endure forever.

PART FIVE

RETURN TO CAMBODIA

CHAPTER 17

I N 1986 GOD called me back to Cambodia, to my hometown of Takéo, to preach the gospel. He spoke clearly to me, but I didn't want to listen. I didn't want to return to Cambodia. Memories of life in prison were still fresh. I could literally smell the odor of communism and that filthy prison cell.

"No, Lord!" I cried. "Forget it! Not me! I don't want to return to Cambodia."

God was persistent, though, and continued to speak to me about Cambodia. One day a letter came in the mail from Pastor Sieng Ang, one of my spiritual fathers in Cambodia. I had not heard from anyone in Cambodia for many years. It had taken six months for Sieng Ang's letter to reach me.

"Come back to Cambodia, son," his letter read. "Come back and preach the gospel; and when you do, Jesus will come back also."

I knew this was confirmation of God's call, but still I resisted. I felt that my family and I were safe and secure in America. The same Vietnamese government that had occupied Cambodia after ousting the Khmer Rouge was still in power. These were the people who had imprisoned me. It wouldn't be safe for me to return and certainly not safe for me to bring my family back with me. As a widower I had no one to leave the children with if I were to go back, so I continued to plant churches and train leadership in America while ignoring God's call to Cambodia.

Long Beach, California, and Stockton, California, had large concentrations of Cambodians, and I was able to plant churches in both cities. We had a nice big building in Stockton and a large, supportive congregation. My children were in good schools, and I was busy overseeing several church plants. It was 1988, and I was still ignoring God's call to Cambodia. But God didn't let me ignore Him forever.

In 1989 He spoke to me again about returning to Cambodia, and this time the call literally shook me physically and emotionally. I was in bed asleep one night when the bed began to shake so violently that it woke me, as well as my two sons who were sleeping in the next room. The bed was literally flying up and down in the air. It was like we were having an earthquake, but it was going on only in my bedroom. Fear gripped me, and my strength left me. I was unable to speak for three days except to talk to the Lord.

I couldn't ignore God any longer. It was obvious that I had to return to Cambodia, but I had no visa or passport, no place to live when I got there, and no money to get me there. I decided to call my friend Mike Hudgins, a Vineyard pastor in Orange County, California. Mike had been discipled by Todd Burke. I first met Mike when he and Todd visited the refugee camps in the early 1980s.

I called Mike and shared with him the visitation from God and His unequivocal call for me to return to Cambodia. Mike and Martin Buehlmann, a Vineyard pastor from Switzerland who today is national director for the Vineyard in Germany, Austria, and Switzerland, were able to arrange for me to preach at a few Vineyard churches in the ensuing weeks to raise awareness and financial support for my return mission to Cambodia.

DEBORAH

One of the people who came to hear me preach was a woman named Deborah. She was a native of Thailand, and her friend Ann thought that Deborah would be interested in my mission work in Cambodia. On the night Deborah came to hear me speak, I had brought quite a few young people with me, including my children. As I began to talk and share my story, Deborah felt God touching her heart, telling her that she would marry me one day. Startled, Deborah dismissed those thoughts.

After the meeting, as we gathered for coffee, Ann introduced me to Deborah. We quickly found that we had much in common. As with me, God had put a fire in Deborah's heart to share the message of the gospel. She had been busy preaching at many of the Laos and Thai churches in and around Los Angeles. That night she felt led to give two hundred dollars to support my mission work.

Just as God was touching Deborah's heart for me, He also was touching my heart for her. He was giving us both a vision that we would join together to serve Him. It was not until later that we found out God had touched our hearts at the same time with the same vision. After our meeting that night, Deborah began to pray for me and my mission work.

During one of the church services a woman was healed of blindness. This lovely church was right by the ocean, with the windows of the sanctuary looking over the water. The woman was standing by the windows during a time of prayer, and the Lord just healed her eyes. This church gave generously to my mission work, enabling me to obtain my visa, passport, and tickets to fly to Cambodia.

After the service a woman named Susan introduced herself. She was the sister of David Yonggi Cho, a prominent Korean pastor. Reverend Cho invited me to speak at his church in Seoul, South Korea, which I did. Reverend Cho's church, Yoido Full Gospel Church, was eager to partner with me and gave generously.

BACK TO CAMBODIA

It was finally time to return to Cambodia. I made arrangements for Kris and Mary Ann Young to care for my children in my absence. This young couple was serving in a Cambodian church in Tacoma, Washington, when I first met them. God put a call on their hearts to support me, and when I moved from Seattle to Stockton, the Youngs moved with me. Later they would join me in ministry in Cambodia.

My plan initially was to be gone no longer than forty days. "If I am gone longer than forty days," I said to Kris and Mary Ann, "my family is yours."

We said our tearful good-byes, and then I boarded the plane for Cambodia with my Bible and six hundred dollars in cash in my pocket. I arrived in Singapore, where I stayed for a week, praying about what to do next. Only one flight a week was going into Cambodia at that time. While in Singapore I was able to speak at several local churches, thanks to YWAM connections.

I was so afraid to return to Cambodia. Memories of prison haunted me. I knew I didn't have the strength to endure imprisonment again. I cried out to the Lord, asking for His protection. I had boldness in the Spirit to return to Cambodia, but my flesh was weak.

After a week in Singapore, I flew into Cambodia. My family picked me up at the airport. I decided to stay at Solomon Church with the remnant of believers still meeting there. Solomon Church had been planted by Todd and DeAnn Burke's main church in Phnom Penh in the early 1970s. The Christian church in Cambodia had been forced underground for ten years, from 1979 to 1989. In 1989 the government made Christianity legal, but many of the churches were slow to recover.

Solomon Church had experienced an amazing visitation of God in the 1970s when He sent His holy fire on the church. God had released His glory in the building. The people literally could see tongues of fire burning everywhere, but nothing was consumed. A fire truck even came at one point, but nothing actually burned.

At the time I had left Cambodia for America, the congregation of Solomon Church was composed largely of widows. I think there were about forty-five widows. These women were strong intercessors, and I found out they had prayed for me the entire time I was away. They had no idea I had been in prison or what had happened to me. They would just sit on the floor and weep and pray for me, asking the Lord to protect me and bless me. Upon my return to Cambodia, they were overjoyed to see me and to hear of everything God had done. Just as Paul in the Bible found a safe haven with the widows, so too did I.

FEED THE POOR, CARE FOR THE ORPHANS

When God called me back to Cambodia, He told me to feed the poor and take care of the orphans. This was a huge challenge. The infrastructure of the country was in ruins, and the people were extremely poor and broken from years of war. They were without hope. I had little money and didn't know how I would feed anyone, but I went forward, acting on what He had told me, trusting Him because I was doing what He had called me to do.

I went into the streets and began to pick up orphans and bring them home. In two days I had seven or eight children. For three months I took care of these children by myself. Then God blessed me. He sent me a group of young people between the ages of fourteen and twenty-five—about eight of them. Together with these young people and the small group of orphans, we began to pray and worship, and God sent His revival fire. Out of these daily prayer meetings God birthed a new church. It was a miracle church.

When the pastor of a local Baptist church, a man named Kakada, heard what was happening at our church, he came with his mother to join us for daily prayer. Each day he would bring his mother and lay her on the floor in front of the prayer room. This went on for about two weeks. Then one morning she just stood up and shouted, "Hallelujah!" She had been unable to walk, and God had healed her.

After that she went from village to village sharing her testimony of healing. That is when God started turning things upside down. As word of her healing spread, our church began to grow. We went from a handful of people to three hundred people and then to six or seven hundred.

CHAPTER 18

ONE DAY THE power and glory of God touched a blind man and his wife in our church, sparking a new wave of revival. The Khmer Rouge had blinded them both, and they had been reduced to begging to survive. Every day their fifteen-year-old son would take his father into the city of Phnom Penh to beg in the streets. At this time the poor were flooding into Phnom Penh. One day the father and his son passed by our church and heard us worshipping.

The father said, "Son, I heard someone singing beautiful songs. Please take me to this singing."

So his son brought him upstairs to the fourth floor of the building where we conducted our church services. Because the presence of God was with us, this man liked sitting in our services. Every day he would have his son take him to beg in the streets in the morning and then bring him to our church in the afternoon. He would sit and listen to the Word of God and the beautiful music. And then one morning, God opened his eyes. He could see again! For seventeen years he had been unable to see. He had never seen his son.

At that time I lived in the church building, which also housed the orphans and our workers. For a month after this man's healing, he stayed with us; then we sent him back to his hometown, Sala Lek Pram, in Kampong Chhnang Province. When he arrived in Sala Lek Pram, he was surrounded by the townspeople as he stood and shared his testimony. Everyone knew of his blindness, and they were amazed at this miracle healing of God.

Our church was able to build a house for this man and his family in Sala Lek Pram, and within a few months they had planted a church in that house. Many hundreds of people have come to know Jesus through this church. This blind man who was healed pastored his church for many years before he stepped down, and his son, who had once led his father through the streets of Phnom Penh to beg, became an anointed pastor, following in his father's footsteps.

Our church continued to grow very quickly. Each day I would go out and feed the poor and care for the orphans. It was a very busy time for me. At that time Cambodia had only two or three TV channels. But even those few channels were very popular because the people were hungry for anything. Each day when I went out to preach the gospel and feed the poor and care for the orphans, two of these TV channels would send crews to follow me. They followed me everywhere, and they would put the footage on the evening news.

KING SIHANOUK HEALED

In 1991 King Sihanouk returned to Cambodia from China, where he had gone into exile after the coup led by General Lon Nol in 1970. About that same time, as a result of a United Nations peacekeeping mission, all the refugees living in the camps along the Thai border were able to return to Cambodia. King Sihanouk, who had heard of my work and knew it was on television for fifteen or twenty minutes every day, began to watch the broadcasts. As he did, God touched his heart. He asked his assistant about me and was told I was part of a Christian group that fed the poor. I had come to know his son, Prince Norodom Ranariddh, who became the first prime minister of Cambodia after the 1993 election sponsored by the United Nations.

King Sihanouk was curious to know where my strength came from—how I was able to care for the poor every day. He wanted to know where the food came from to feed so many. Prince Ranariddh came to me and asked if I would meet with his father. When I agreed, he arranged a meeting for the very next day.

That night as I lay sleeping, God gave me a dream in which I saw myself meeting with the king. In the dream I was sitting next to the king. God also showed me a beautiful woman, although I could not see her face. In the dream, He was drawing this beautiful woman close to me. I awoke to the ringing of the telephone. It was Deborah calling to pray with me. My heart felt like it would burst from my chest at the sound of her voice. Could she be the beautiful woman in the dream whom God was drawing close to me?

Having been out in the province, I was not very presentable. I was in need of a shower and a haircut and a gift of flowers to bring to the king, but there was no opportunity for any of that before the meeting. I had to go as I was.

In Cambodia when anyone would go to see the king, a certain protocol was to be followed. Visitors would be escorted into the throne room, the king would sit on his throne, and his visitors sat, according to protocol, off to the side. No one ever sat in front of the king or next to him. When I arrived at the throne room, the door was open. As I approached, the king came out.

He stepped down, and reaching out for my hand, he said, "Sophal?"

Bowing down, I answered, "Yes."

Still holding my hand, he began to lead me toward the throne; as we got to the throne, he beckoned for me to sit beside him, just like I had seen in the dream.

As I sat next to him, he looked at me and said, "Son, I love what you are doing here. Every time I watch you on television, I have many questions that I want to ask you."

We began to talk, and I told him that the work I was doing was because God had told me to feed the poor and care for the orphans. As he questioned me about where the food came from and where I got the money to feed the poor, I was able to share the gospel with him. For about an hour I took him through the Old and New Testaments. He listened patiently and then asked if there were a lot of Christians in the world. When I told him yes, there were a lot of Christians all over the world, he asked me if I would bring them all to Cambodia to rebuild the country!

With his permission, I began to pray for him. I told him that God had opened a door for Cambodia because He wanted to heal this country that had been cursed by war and genocide. I told him God wanted to bless him, as king, with wisdom to lead the country. He was most eager to receive this blessing from God. As we prayed, I told him to give his heart to God and to cry out to Him for Cambodia. And then, with great joy, he received a Bible, a real Khmer Bible.

It was then that King Sihanouk shared with me that he had brain cancer. He was in poor health from the cancer and traveled to China every six months for treatment. I told him about Jesus, the King of kings and the Doctor of doctors, and that the Bible tells us Jesus heals us of every sickness and disease if we will come to Him in repentance, seeking His forgiveness. Then I offered to pray for his healing. With his permission, I laid my hands on him and asked God to heal him of the cancer and to strengthen him so that he, as king, could help bring healing and restoration to Cambodia.

About six months later I received a beautiful letter from King Sihanouk. It began with the words "Thank you." He told me of the peace and joy that had come into his life with Jesus and that Jesus had healed him of the brain cancer. It was a beautiful letter to the glory of God, and I took it with me everywhere and shared it as often as I could. Many in the Cambodian Christian community began to request copies of the letter.

With the king's permission, a thousand copies of the letter were reprinted in newspapers and magazines—wherever it could be printed—so that as many people as possible could hear the good news and know the glory of God. God continued to bless our efforts in Cambodia.

With solid leadership in place in the church, I returned to the United States. Within seven years the Cambodian leaders I had raised up were able to plant churches in every province as God called us to do, and each new church plant experienced a miracle.

MARRIAGE

In 1992 I made plans to move to Cambodia permanently and to bring Pheakdey and Makara with me. The friendship between me and Deborah continued to grow and deepen until it became obvious that we were to marry. It is customary in our culture for parents to arrange the marriages of their children, so my mother approached Deborah about marrying me, and she quickly agreed. We were married in 1992, and God blessed our marriage with a son. He spoke clearly to

Deborah during her pregnancy and told her to name him Daniel, saying that he would be God's vessel to be used for His glory.

Since our wedding God has been using us powerfully as a team to bring the light of the gospel to those still caught in darkness in Cambodia and elsewhere. With hearts united by a passion to see the lost saved and set free, we have continued to experience the power of God since the day we said our vows. Every day brings something new. The challenges remain, but they are nothing compared to the rewards that are known in heaven.

PART SIX

A NEW SEASON

CHAPTER 19

I AM SO THANKFUL that God brought Deborah into my life. Even though I have experienced great loss and persecution, my heart still burns for Jesus. Together Deborah and I have been able to accomplish so much more than I would have accomplished alone, as a widower. When two people are joined in holy love, Jesus, by His Holy Spirit, comes to them, making a threefold cord that is not easily broken (Eccles. 4:12).

Our gifts and talents are different, but together Deborah and I complement each other. Deborah ministers under a strong anointing with healing miracles and salvations. She has a radio program that reaches many who otherwise would not hear the lifesaving message of Jesus. God has used us mightily since our marriage in 1992.

THE CHURCH IN BATTAMBANG

In 1995 God sent Deborah and me to the northwest Cambodian province of Battambang. As I mentioned earlier, it was the only province we were given permission to minister in, outside the city of Phnom Penh. During the occupation Battambang was a major Khmer Rouge stronghold and one of their main killing fields. It was a very broken place after the war. God led us to Battambang to plant another church, and everything about that church plant was a miracle; it was like something straight out of the Bible.

Before the war my younger brother Samoeum had planted a church in Battambang, and out of that church six other house churches grew. When the Khmer Rouge came, they killed my brother. His body died, but I know his spirit is with the Lord. A strong anointing remained in Battambang despite the efforts of the Khmer Rouge.

At the time Deborah and I were called there, I had no intention of planting a church in that province. I was busy traveling from our home church in Phnom Penh—going all around the country, from province to province, visiting different churches. One of our stops was in Chhnang, at the church where the blind man was healed, and one was in Pursat, where I received my first call from God. God had given me the church in Pursat many years before, and I had finally returned to train the people there.

After a week of training in Pursat my two traveling companions and I felt it was time to return home. Men of God, we had very little money between us, barely enough for gasoline for the car trip home. The church in Cambodia is very poor. Churches there are not like churches in America, where the members support the pastor. In Cambodia the pastor supports the members. It is a country of extreme poverty.

The morning before we were to leave, I woke up quite early, about four o'clock in the morning. Lying in my bed, I began to shake; and as I lay shaking, I had a clear vision. I heard the Lord say, "Go forward and do not go backward. Go north toward Thailand, and then you will be able to come back home. Go straight. Go toward Thailand." I couldn't understand how we could go forward because we didn't have any money, but I knew I was hearing clearly from God. In obedience we drove north for about two hours over very poor roads until we found ourselves in Battambang.

We arrived on a Friday evening, and by Sunday I was preaching in the pulpit of a local Methodist church. The Spirit of God was strong that day, and many young people and leaders came under the conviction of the Holy Spirit.

We felt a strong leading that this was the place we were to plant a church. By the grace of God we found an affordable property to rent. In short order God provided a pastor and a worship leader. In the power of the Spirit this church plant grew to more than three hundred people in four years.

Together Deborah and I ministered powerfully in Battambang. When our lease was up, the owners found it necessary to increase the rent beyond what we could afford, and we were forced to look for a new location for our church. We prayed, and God led us to a parcel next to a highway. However, the owners were asking far more than we could afford. Feeling like we were to stay in Battambang, we went to our knees in prayer, asking God for His provision.

Not long after that I was invited to speak at a church in Dallas, Texas. I flew back to the United States, and standing in the pulpit that Sunday, I shared my vision of the piece of land along the highway in Battambang. The Dallas church caught the vision, and with their blessing I was able to return to Cambodia with enough money to approach the owners of the property. They accepted my offer—another miracle of God! We had arrived in Battambang with not even enough gas money to return home, and no idea why we were there, and now we owned a piece of land for a church, paid in full!

Within a year of purchasing the land, we were able by God's grace to build a church and an orphanage on the property without one penny of debt. The Battambang church seats one thousand people, and the orphanage houses two hundred children. We call it the Church on the Way. Within two years we had planted seventeen new house churches in the surrounding villages.

My experience of the power of God to build His church in Battambang has never left me. Our simple act of obedience resulted in a rich harvest for the kingdom. We had nothing, yet all the Lord needed from us was our obedience. He provided the rest.

PLANTING CHURCHES IN AND AROUND PHNOM PENH

When Deborah and I left the United States and returned to war-ravaged Cambodia, it was not hard to find the poor, the hungry, and the orphans, but many people found it too difficult to care for them. We chose not to focus on what man could not do, but instead I simply trusted God for what He would do.

When we first returned to the city of Phnom Penh, we were not allowed to have a church building. We met in house churches until the government gave us what had once been a Catholic primary school before the Khmer Rouge came to power. Pol Pot, the Khmer Rouge dictator, had been a student at that school. The building was not ideal for a church. It consisted of mostly small classrooms, but to us it was a huge blessing.

We spent five or six years in that building, and our congregation grew to more than a thousand. We were holding two or three services a day and had to meet on the fourth floor, as it had the only space large enough to accommodate our services. It was not easy for many in our congregation to make the climb up and down the stairs. I knew we needed more space, and as I prayed, God gave me His vision of the land we were to buy in Phnom Penh. The land was to be big enough to hold a large church with a large first-floor sanctuary.

At the time that God gave me this vision, about 90 percent of our congregation were from the slums. These people were very poor, and most had no money. Weekly tithes and offerings just barely covered utilities.

I knew that any money for this vision would have to come from the Lord.

LAND OF OUR OWN

I scoured the city for land but couldn't find anything that appeared suitable. Deborah and I realized that the only way we would find land was to get on our knees, and so we commenced to fast and pray for three months. And then one day we saw it—an old army base, dirty, overgrown, and littered with machine guns. In the natural it didn't look like the right place for a church, but with God's vision it began to look like the soil of heaven to me. Every morning for three months I would go there and pray. I got to the point where I really wanted that piece of land.

It took a while for Deborah to catch the vision for the property, but when she did, the two of us, in one accord, took it before the leadership of our congregation. With their agreement, we then approached the owner of the property. He was willing to sell, but his price was way beyond what we had to offer, and he wanted cash.

Because I knew that the Lord had already put this land on my heart, I persisted, explaining that even though I didn't have all the money at that time, I was certain God would provide the rest of it for me. I told him that if he would accept my deposit, God would send the remainder of the money soon. Even though he had never done anything like that before, he finally agreed to hold the land for us for one month, with our five-hundred-dollar deposit—which was all the money this poor pastor had in the world.

A couple of days later a friend invited me to speak at his church in Australia. It was very short notice, but I felt that God wanted me to go, so I agreed and soon was on a plane.

The first night in Australia I spoke to more than one hundred young people. I had been speaking for only about five minutes when wind hit me. I was standing on the platform, and a wind began to blow with such force that it knocked me down. I wasn't sure what had happened. As I looked out over the crowd, I saw that all the young people were down too. They had fallen all over the chairs. When God wants to do something, He just does it. I didn't have to do anything.

Later I was told that I had been picked up by members of the church, put in a car, and driven to the home of a brother named Oscar, where I awoke in the wee hours of the morning. Oscar told me this was the first time these teenagers had received the baptism of the Holy Spirit. They had started speaking in tongues, and the noise had filled the church. They were still at the church, out in the power of the Spirit.

And then he said to me, "By the way, look in your pockets. I saw a pastor put a check in your pocket."

Sure enough, there was a check in my pocket. Glory to God! With this new blessing in hand, I headed home to Cambodia, and Deborah and I went straight to the owner of the old army base and gave him what we had promised, holding back 10 percent as a tithe. He was astounded and agreed to continue to work with us.

God provided the remainder of the funding through a young man named Greg, from Texas. He and his wife owned a successful furniture business in Texas, and they felt strongly that the Lord wanted them to give us their income-tax refund. It was the first year they hadn't owed taxes. It was another miracle! When the check arrived, Deborah and I went straight to the owner of our "promised land" property again. Holding back our 10 percent tithe, we were able to make another payment on the land. The owner of the property was shocked. Long story short, we paid off the land in a year.

This man was a Buddhist, but he was so impressed with our God that he reduced the price of the property. He told me how he and his wife had given a lot away to Buddha. They had built a temple and housing for a monk. They had been content as Buddhists, but when they met me and saw God move powerfully, they wanted to know more. I was able to share the gospel with them, and even though they didn't abandon their Buddhist faith, God worked through them to grow the church in Cambodia.

A Building for Our Land

With the land now ours, we continued to pray, and God gave us a vision for the building that was to go on the land. In this vision I saw a huge building, in great detail. I'm not an engineer or an architect, but

I saw a picture of what the building was to look like, and I began to draw it in precise detail. I worked for three weeks on the drawing and then submitted it to an architectural firm, requesting that they draw up plans to match my drawing exactly.

With building plans in hand, our church began to pray—every day from five thirty to seven o'clock in the morning. Three hundred of us prayed, shouted, and thanked the Lord. There were many pastors and leaders among us. One day I asked someone to hold up the architectural plans in front of the congregation. Standing next to the worship team, I looked out at the people and said, "Who among you wants a building like this?" The reply was a resounding, "We do!"

I invited everyone to come forward and put their money and whatever else they had to give in the offering plate. They gave all they had. Some of them put gold in the offering plate. Even though we were a very poor congregation, the people gave five thousand dollars that day. It is not easy to ask for money from poor people. It was God's grace that allowed them to give it.

Some of them wrote letters that touched my heart deeply. One person wrote, "Father, I saved this money for five years, but when you spoke about the building, I wanted to give to help build a foundation for the kingdom of God in Cambodia." They were so poor that it had taken them five years to save the money—and they gave it all to God. We received several hundred letters in all. These people gave everything they had.

I hired a construction company to begin work, and even though we encountered all sorts of obstacles, God overcame every one of them. In nine short months the building was completed, and we were able to pay it off soon afterward.

With the building completed, we began to pray for God's provision for the remainder of what was needed. We needed chairs, a sound system, and all kinds of other things. The chairs were the first to be provided by a small Vineyard house church in Southern California. Next came the sound system and everything else we needed, from another Vineyard church in California. Within a year the building was complete. Since the day we opened our doors, the church has grown to overflowing. Everything about it was a miracle, from start to finish. And God deserves all the glory!

In addition to the church, we eventually were able to build an adjoining orphanage. We also were able to construct another large church in Sihanoukville Province thanks to God's continued miraculous provision. Nothing is impossible with God. He will build His church!

CHAPTER 20

URING THE 1990s two governments in Cambodia, the Funcinpec Party and the Cambodian People's Party (CPP)—headed by former Khmer Rouge who had defected and turned to Vietnam for support to topple the Khmer Rouge—fought against each other. Headed by the Hun Sen family, the CPP staged a coup in 1997 and managed to regain power. Some of the worst fighting was in the city of Phnom Penh. Night and day the violence continued, killing hundreds.

Our church in Phnom Penh became a place of refuge. Many people flocked to our building to escape the violence. God gave me His miraculous provision of a large truck. It was a huge, powerful truck with God's anointing on it. The government gave me a special license plate so that I could drive anywhere in the city. I had authority from God and I had authority from the government. My heart was breaking for my congregation, many of whom were stranded throughout the city. Sometimes family members would make it to the safety of the church, while the rest of their family remained behind. That's when I would go out with the truck and pick up people and bring them back to the safety of the church.

Our son Daniel was four years old at the time, just a small child. The three of us, Deborah, Daniel, and I, would often go out together, into the midst of the violence. We tried to stay together as a family whenever possible so that if something happened we would be together.

The streets of Phnom Penh were littered with bodies. We knew the importance of getting people to safety, so we went out again and again, bringing people back to the church. At one point we had more than four hundred people staying in the church. They lived on rice and water. We had eighty-four rooms on five floors, enough space to house between four hundred and five hundred people. No one knew how long the war would go on.

SAVED FROM DEATH AGAIN

My friend Norodom Ranariddh, first prime minister of Cambodia, was ousted by the military coup led by the co-prime minister, Hun Sen, in 1997. He fled the country until 1998 when he returned to form a new coalition with Hun Sen. He later went on to form what is now the third largest political party in Cambodia, the Norodom Ranariddh Party.

During the coup, the city fell silent and the streets were empty. A message arrived at the church, written on the back of a business card. It was from the secretary of state for the Funcinpec Party. This three-star general was trapped in the Singapore Embassy in the middle of the city. The message scrawled on the back of the card read: "Brother Sophal, please help me. I got stuck here in Singapore Embassy, but there are no people here. Only me and my friend in the building."

I knew this man. He had worked for me twenty years ago, before he was called to government service where he eventually became secretary of state. When the military coup took over the city, he was stranded in the embassy.

Deborah and I jumped in the truck and drove straight to the embassy. It was eerily silent when we arrived. My friend and his companion had been hiding in the garden, and when they heard our big truck arrive, they came out of the bushes and climbed in. They were weak and dirty from two or three days without food.

"What do you want me to do?" I asked him. "Where do you want me to take you, brother?"

He replied, "Brother Sophal, wherever you go, I want to go with you. In death and life I want to go with you. I want to go to your church with you."

At that time his five children, whom we had rescued, were sheltered at the church with us. My first thought was to take him to the Cambodian Hotel because I knew it was a safe place. Foreign teams were staying there, waiting to get out of the country. Nobody was allowed to attack the hotel, and I felt it would be the safest place for him. I knew that if the new government found him, they would probably kill him. But he didn't want to go to the hotel. He wanted to go to our church, so that's where we headed.

As we drove away from the embassy, I put him and his friend in the backseat of the truck, and we began to pray over them in tongues. They looked terrible, almost like dead people.

After driving only about half a mile, we approached a four-way intersection. In the intersection was a large group of special-forces soldiers, about twenty of them. As we drove through, they surrounded the truck. I kept driving, and they began to chase us, making signs for me to slow down and stop. I stopped the truck, and several soldiers approached and began to explain what they wanted.

"We know we have no authority over your vehicle, and we aren't interested in you," one soldier said to me. "We want the two men in the back of your truck."

With that, they opened the back doors, jumped in the truck, and handcuffed both men.

"Drive back to the Ministry of Interior," they commanded me.

With an escort of about twenty motorcycles, which looked like the motorcade used to escort the king, we took off. Sirens wailing, we went through the silent streets of the city. Upon arriving at the ministry building, they shoved the two men in the backseat out the door and into the building, into a room. Then they took me and put me in another room, and Deborah in a third room. Frightened, I cried out, "Lord, help us!"

Deborah told me later that they came into her room and asked who I was. When she told them I was her husband, they came and got me and began to interrogate both of us. Surrounded by soldiers with machine guns, they asked us questions and wrote everything down. As I looked at these men, I saw their eyes were bloodshot and evil. Again I prayed, "Lord, I need Your help!" Because Deborah could not speak Khmer, I had to translate for her.

I told them I was a man of God and that I ran an organization that fed the poor and cared for orphans. I told them that when the war came, people came to me asking for help. They wanted to come to our building because it was safe. I told them I would go out with my truck and bring people back to our church.

"How about the two men in the back of your truck?" they asked. "Do they work for you?"

"No," I replied. "I knew one of these men a long time ago. His son and daughter attend our church. When he asked me for help, I helped him. I wanted to take him to the hotel, but he insisted I take him to our church instead."

With that, the soldiers left. I sensed the presence of evil very strongly, and I felt I was to go into the room where the two men were being held. I knew there was a refrigerator in there, probably with water in it, and so I asked for some water. The soldiers directed me into the next room and sure enough, there were my friend and his companion, chained to their chairs. As soon as they saw me, they said, "Brother Sophal, don't come in here. Get out! Something bad is about to happen."

I took water from the refrigerator and said to my friend, "Brother, here is water, healing water in the name of Jesus. Bless this man, Lord."

As he drank the water we prayed, and then I quickly left the room and went back to Deborah in the next room. Suddenly we heard the sound of machine guns— twenty, maybe thirty rounds of machine-gun fire. Deborah fell to the floor.

"What just happened?" I asked the soldier who was guarding us.

"Nothing," he replied. "Don't worry about it. Everything is fine."

I knew at that moment that they had killed my friend and his companion. Fearing for our own lives, I remembered a picture I had in my wallet. It was a picture of the president and his wife, all the government leaders and ministers, and me and Deborah. The picture had been taken several years before, soon after Deborah and I were married and had returned to Cambodia from America. He was president of the CPP. Deborah and I had been invited to the palace to dine with him. I always carried this picture with me in my wallet.

I looked at Deborah on the floor, with tears streaming down her face. In the midst of her fear I saw her faith and the glory of God shining on her face. At that moment God gave me boldness and a word. Taking the picture out of my wallet, I handed it to the soldiers standing over us with machine guns.

I said, "Brothers, see this picture of the president and the ministers of the National Assembly and the heads of state with me and my wife? I worked with this president. I built a school for him in his home province. He told me that my wife and I were like a son and daughter to him."

Then I showed him another little picture in my wallet of me with the president and his wife, and Sar Kheng, the minister of interior.

"Oh, this is my minister, my boss," replied the soldier.

Taking the picture from my hand, he ran out of the room and up the stairs. The room was silent except for Deborah's weeping. The glory was all over her. Finally the soldier returned with the picture. As it turned out, this soldier was the right-hand man to the minister of interior.

Handing the picture to me, he said, "Brother Sophal, I know now that you take care of orphans and feed the poor. Please tell your wife that I am so sorry for holding you so long. We only wanted the bad men in the back of your truck. You are free to go back home now. I have no more issues with you."

"Let's leave this evil place immediately!" Deborah whispered to me.

We were escorted to our truck and drove away from that place as fast as we could, straight back to the church, praising God all the way for saving us. When we arrived at the church, we saw four big military motorcycles outside. I didn't know if the soldiers were there to protect us or to spy on us. I sent one of our orphan sons to ask them why they were there. He brought word back to me that they were there to protect us. God had sent four bodyguards to protect us in our church!

That night Deborah and I couldn't sleep. We just lay in bed shaking and fearful at the thought that we had almost died. They had killed two men in the room next to us, and it only made sense that they would have killed us too, to silence us. We knew that all over the country people had been killed, important government people and people in high places. Regardless of their status, they had been brutally murdered. The soldiers who had stood over us with machine guns did not think twice about killing, yet God had spared us and set us free.

DELIVERED FROM EVIL

It wasn't the only time that God spared our lives. One day Deborah and I were driving near the airport, and the baby was in the truck with us. We had just picked up some people and were heading back to the church when I happened to see an airplane on fire. I had a little camera with me, and I stopped the truck to get out and take a picture. As I did, I heard loud noises behind me, and when I turned to look, I saw about ten army tanks bearing down on my truck, where Deborah and the baby were still inside. With machine guns at the ready, a tank rammed the truck. A bullet from one of the tanks hit the seat of the truck. Miraculously no one was hurt, and the truck was not damaged other than the bullet hole in the seat.

I raced back and jumped in the truck. I tried to start the engine, but it wouldn't turn over. Another tank pulled up in front of me. Now we had one in front and one behind. I think the tank that pulled up in front was going to ram us, but God must have stopped it because it stalled. I could see the eyes of the men inside, red and full of evil.

I tried a second time to start the truck; the engine roared to life and off we went. Both tanks were stalled and couldn't follow us. With my foot to the floorboard, I drove as fast as I could. Bodies littered the streets, and I couldn't help but run over many of them. We made it back to the safety of the church. God had saved us once again.

CHAPTER 21

MANY THINGS HAPPENED for the kingdom as a result of my friendship with Norodom Ranariddh, the most important being that I was able to lead him to the Lord. He gave his life to Jesus Christ, but because he was prime minister, he was not allowed to attend church. Occasionally he would invite me to his home to share the gospel. His family also heard the message of the gospel, and some accepted Christ. Most of the time all I could do was pray for this man and his family because they could not attend church.

When God opened the door for the gospel to come legally into Cambodia, I began planting churches. From 1991 to 1994 I planted churches. Deborah labored alongside me after our marriage in 1992. I would visit these church plants on a regular basis.

At one point, in 1994, I held a leadership meeting at our home church. Sixty to seventy church leaders came. We talked and prayed and came into agreement with what God was doing in Cambodia. Out of that meeting came the idea for a crusade, but we knew we needed the government's help.

THE PHNOM PENH CRUSADE

Knowing that I had a deep friendship with Prince Ranariddh, the leadership committee appointed me as the person to talk with him to try to secure his permission to use the large stadium in Phnom Penh for our crusade. The prince received me warmly and allowed me to share my vision with him.

"It's long past time for a crusade in this city," I said. "Would you consider granting us permission to use the stadium?"

"This crusade is a fine idea, and you have my support," he replied. "However, the stadium is in a state of serious disrepair. It hasn't been used since the Khmer Rouge era. The lights don't work, and the restrooms aren't functional. It's a mess."

Not knowing where the money would come from, I boldly replied, "We'll take care of all the necessary repairs if you'll grant us permission to use the stadium."

Prince Ranariddh gave us the use of the stadium free of charge. I went back to the leadership committee with the good news, and we began to get estimates on the needed repairs. The final estimate to fix everything was high, and of course we didn't have that kind of money, but God did.

I began to go out and talk to various people. One of them was a friend in Bangkok, a pastor and an engineer. When I shared my needs with him, he said, "Sophal, I'll tell you what. I will send an engineer, electricians, and workers to fix everything. We'll put everything right for you. The fact that you have no money is not an issue."

He sent his people from Bangkok a month later, and they fixed everything. They cleaned, painted, put the bathrooms in working order, and repaired the lights. They gave us large, strong stadium lights. The work was completed in about two months' time. They knew Cambodia was a poor country and that the church had no money, but they also knew God was opening the country to the gospel, and they wanted to help.

This pastor from Bangkok not only was a man of God and an engineer but also had once been a famous actor in Thailand. He had a beautiful, powerful singing voice. After he gave his life to Jesus, the Lord used his powerful voice to lead worship. He knew the importance of a good sound system, and he provided one for us.

With the stadium in good repair, I began going around the city, gathering the signatures that would be needed for the crusade to go forward. In two days I had all the signatures I needed. The Holy Spirit pushed me hard for those two days. I knocked on doors until late into the night. Several times people asked me, "Why don't you just wait until morning?"

"I have too much to do, and there isn't time," I replied. "When God speaks, I obey and He provides!"

GOD'S GLORY AND A GRAPHIC VISION

God provided Mike Evans, a journalist and founder of the Jerusalem Prayer Team, as our main speaker, as well as a worship team and an intercessory prayer team. We had about five thousand leaders. I gathered them together for a week of training. We trained for eighteen hours a day, from seven in the morning till midnight.

The first night of the crusade, about one hundred thousand people came, according to our estimate. They crowded down on the field, covering it almost entirely. The stadium seats about fifty thousand on benches, so between the people who crowded into the stands and those who stood on the field, we were able to preach to a crowd double the size of what that stadium normally would hold.

Estimates were that about ten thousand people got saved that first night. Thirty people were asked to come onto the platform to give their testimonies of being healed. Some of them had been carried in as cripples and walked out healed. Many others had been so sick they were not able to walk in on their own, but they walked out healed. The healings continued every day of the crusade.

Years before this crusade, in 1986 while I was living in America, God gave me a vision. In it I saw myself preaching to a large crowd. I was standing in the very same stadium in which we were now holding the crusade, only I didn't know it was that stadium at the time of the vision. I saw myself preaching for several days. On the last day, as things were drawing to a close, I looked to the east and heard something that sounded like a strong earthquake. And then I saw a large man. He was very tall—his head reached almost to the sky. I had never seen this man before. When he walked, the earth shook. It felt like an earthquake.

When I looked in his eyes, I heard him say, "Where is Sophal?" I saw that he had a weapon in one hand, a big machine gun. Again his voice boomed out, "Where is Sophal?" Fear entered my heart, and I went and hid with the intercessory team. A third time he cried out, "Where is Sophal?" And then he saw me, even though I was hiding. He pointed his gun at me, and I knew he wanted to shoot.

"Lord, help me!" I cried. "Help me!" I was terrified.

"Go away!" I commanded, but he just stood there, ready to kill me.

I didn't understand this very graphic vision when God gave it to me in 1986. It wasn't until the second-to-last night of the 1994 crusade that I understood what God was trying to tell me in 1986.

On that night, while I was still at home preparing for the evening service, I received a call from the stadium. Policemen had come and locked the stadium doors.

About seven or eight thousand people were inside the stadium at the time. These people had come from outlying provinces and had no place to stay during the night. We had allowed them to stay inside the stadium, but the police had forced them to leave.

Deborah and I drove quickly to the stadium to talk with the police, but they wouldn't tell me anything.

"What is going on?" I asked.

"You'll have to talk with the minister of interior," was the reply.

We drove quickly to the minister's office, where I explained that we had permission from the prime minister for this crusade. "Everything is in order," I said.

"It's not a problem on your end," they replied. "We had a bomb scare at the stadium. The police had to clear the place out and lock the doors. We caught the people, with bombs strapped to their bodies. We believe they are Khmer Rouge."

We heard reports later that some believed the bombers were Cambodian nationals opposed to Christianity. One report said it was a Buddhist effort to shut us down.

God Will Not Be Thwarted

We had two days left of the crusade, but I was unable to convince the authorities to allow us to reopen the stadium. They allowed us to have a small gathering that day. If there were no problems with it, then they would allow us to hold another small gathering the following day.

"We'll check each of the seven thousand or so people who were in the stadium overnight, and if they are clear, we'll let them back in—but no one else," they offered. "It will take us about four or five hours to check everyone."

The police didn't even want me to return to my house for fear of a bomb going off there. They wanted to escort me to a large hotel in Cambodia and leave me there with twenty guards.

With a heavy heart, I gathered together some leaders and we prayed. I went back to the stadium to check on the sound system and the worship leaders and the team, but the policemen would not let me in. We ended up at the hotel.

In our room we knelt in prayer. At about eight o'clock in the evening, a hundred or so people gathered in front of the hotel. They were chanting, "Oh, Christian, you are not good. You are not good. You are not good, Christian!" I think they were Buddhists.

It was at that point that I understood the fullness of the vision the Lord had given me back in 1986 in America. The enemy wanted to stop God, but nobody can stop the Holy Spirit.

God healed hundreds of people during that crusade, and many gave their lives to Christ and were touched powerfully. What we wanted to do in that stadium in the natural, but couldn't, God accomplished by His Spirit. The people didn't need to be in that stadium for two more nights to be touched by God—He found them all over Cambodia and touched them right where they were. Reports of healings and the fire of the Spirit burning brightly continued to come to us for months after the crusade. We were able to send out workers to follow up with people. God's purposes were not thwarted.

The power of God is real. When He speaks, we need to listen. The problem is not that we don't hear Him. The problem is that we are often disobedient. I was disobedient in America. I wanted to stay there—in a safe place with my family. In my disobedience I didn't trust the Lord to take care of me.

Perhaps He would have used someone else to bring the gospel into Cambodia if I had refused to go, but I don't know that. What I do know is that when I was obedient and returned to Cambodia, God used me.

CHAPTER 22

THE CAMBODIAN PEOPLE'S Party coup of 1997 forced us to leave Cambodia. Deborah, Daniel, and I were able to escape to the Thai border but could go no farther. We had no visas, and my passport had expired. All the embassies had been shut down. We made our way to the airport, and for several days all we could do was wait in the airport.

The price to fly out on a private charter plane was exorbitant, and we had no money, so we just waited and prayed there in the airport with our little boy. Eventually an officer from the Ministry of Interior approached us. As he came close, I saw that he was one of the officers who had killed my friend and his companion in the embassy.

He was quite friendly, and when he learned of our situation, he arranged clearance for us on a government plane. Despite some issues with my passport, which God overcame, we were able to fly out of the country. Hundreds of other people were stuck in that airport, but God got us on a plane and flew us out of Cambodia to Thailand.

Without a proper visa, we didn't know how I would be allowed to stay in Thailand. Deborah was OK because she had a Thai passport, and Daniel was OK because he was born in Bangkok; but I was Cambodian, and the Thai government would not allow me to enter without the proper paperwork. My American reentry permit was worthless, since it had expired. All we could do was go by faith. We prayed on the plane, and an hour later we landed in Bangkok.

TO AMERICA AGAIN

Despite our best efforts, I learned I would not be allowed entry to Thailand. All we could do was wait and pray in the Bangkok airport. Days went by. Our clothes were dirty, we were tired, but still we prayed. And then the power of God hit the Cambodian Embassy.

A friend of mine who worked at the embassy located us at the airport, and with his help I was able to get the necessary paperwork. My passport and visa were renewed, and like VIPs we left the airport in an embassy vehicle. Glory to God! He had done it again. Even though I had no valid passport or visa and we had no money, God got me, my wife, and our son out of Cambodia.

Once in Bangkok I looked up Prince Ranariddh who was then living in Thailand in exile. He invited me immediately to come to his house. When he heard of our predicament, he suggested Deborah and Daniel remain in Thailand while I returned to America. His suggestion was a wise one, and Deborah agreed.

We were able to find suitable lodging at the Bangkok Christian Guesthouse, and with my family safely settled, I headed to America to meet with our Christian brothers and sisters and seek the Lord about what He would have us do. I didn't know if there was much we could do in Bangkok, due to the war.

Divine Appointments in Los Angeles

I flew nonstop to Los Angeles, and on the advice of my son-in-law, I made arrangements for the two of us to attend a large conference in Kansas City. During our second day there I was privileged to meet three mighty men of God: Jack Deere, Wes Campbell, and Mike Bickle.

Jack Deere is a pastor, theologian, and former associate professor of Old Testament at Dallas Seminary. Wes Campbell and his wife, Stacey, are the founders of RevivalNOW! Ministries; they preach and teach globally and work with mercy organizations helping children at risk. Mike Bickle founded and leads the International House of Prayer in Kansas City,

Missouri, as well as overseeing several ministries and a Bible school.

I was given a third-row seat at the conference. Prophetic minister Paul Cain spoke the first day. About fifteen minutes into his talk, he stopped and said, "Oh, I nearly forgot, there is someone here from Cambodia, Sophal Ung. The Lord has told me that I am supposed to pray for him and his wife."

At that I stood up and said, "I'm here, I'm here! I'm right here. I'm the one!" He prayed, and I was most grateful for this community of believers who were coming around me.

The next day I sat with Wes and Jack. At break time Wes invited me for coffee. On the way to the coffee shop, we ran into John Paul Jackson, who proceeded to pray for me. Jackson, who passed away in 2015, was an author, speaker, teacher, and founder of Streams Ministries and moved strongly in the prophetic. That very morning the Lord had spoken to him, telling him he would run into me and was to lay hands on me and pray.

He prayed in tongues, and when he finished I fell to the sidewalk under a powerful anointing. This meeting with John Paul Jackson confirmed in my heart that the Lord had indeed brought me to America on a divine appointment.

During one session Jack taught on what it means to be a leader. He talked about the suffering involved in leadership. His message touched my heart, and I couldn't keep from weeping. I wept throughout his talk and all the way back to my hotel room. His talk touched me so deeply because it was my story. I know the suffering involved in leadership.

The conference lasted five days, and during that time God gave me so much. I was dry, and God refreshed me and filled me up. I met many old friends—pastors who knew me long ago. We were able to spend time together and fellowship together. I shared my current situation with them: how I could not go back to Cambodia and that my wife and son were in Thailand. I told them of my broken heart for the Cambodian people who were suffering so greatly. I told them of the thousands of Cambodian refugees amassing on the Thai border, maybe twenty-five to thirty thousand of them. I shared my heart for wanting to help them, feed them, and preach the gospel to them, and for wanting to set them free in the name of the Lord Jesus Christ.

God Comes in a Mighty Wind

On the last day of the conference we moved from the large meeting hall to a theater. Paul Cain was the speaker again. At one point, I don't know why, but Mike and some of the other leaders invited me to stand up and speak. The meeting room was much like an indoor stadium, in which the speaker is on a platform in the middle and the people are seated around him.

I got up to speak and had been talking for about five minutes when a mighty wind began to blow through the room. It hit me and knocked me from the platform to the floor. I fell hard. Then the Holy Spirit began to speak to the people and they were powerfully touched, all five thousand of them.

I don't know how long I was on the floor, but when I woke up, I saw that some of the leaders had come in humility to wash my feet. "The Lord told me to wash your feet," said one dear black brother as he knelt before me.

The foot washing started with the leaders and spread throughout the room. I looked and saw people lining up. They were washing each other's feet too, using what they had—glasses of water. A long line formed in front of me. For hours, pastors and leaders came through the line, wanting to talk with me and wash my feet. One by one I spoke with each of them. Some who could not wait any longer gave my son-in-law their business cards.

The next day I met with Jack, Wes, and several of the other leaders over breakfast. They were very encouraging. I asked for prayers for my grief over not being in Cambodia. I told them that I loved my nation and the refugees there and of how much I wanted to go back. At one point Wes received a word from the Lord for me.

"The Lord wants you to know that even though you are not physically with your people right now, you are with them in spirit," he said. "The Holy Spirit keeps you connected."

"You Need to Write a Book"

Wes was not the only one with a word for me. Throughout the conference people came to me with words from God. One night Wes knocked on the door of my hotel room. We sat and talked and prayed, and even called Deborah so he could talk with her.

"You need to write a book," he said. "I know you don't have the time, but we can get someone to help you if you'd like."

He left, and about thirty minutes later Jack knocked on my door. It must have been close to midnight. He too wanted to call Deborah and encourage her, and so we did. And then he told me that I needed to write a book!

Jack left, and then along came Mike. He prayed with me, and we called Deborah again. And then he too told me that I needed to write a book. God had sent three of His mighty men to my room on the same night to tell me to write a book!

The next morning others came to me and talked about a book. Finally, I said, "OK, God, if I have time I'll write a book."

After that conference I began to receive invitations to speak at churches all over the country. I told the Lord I was willing but that I needed to return to Thailand soon, to be with Deborah and our young son.

As I prayed over the list of invitations, the Holy Spirit highlighted two churches for me. One was a Vineyard church in Portland, Oregon. The pastor's name was

Arian. I had never heard of the church, but my heart was touched.

I was able to speak and minister at both churches before leaving the United States. I talked about how God had brought me out of war-torn Cambodia and of the work we were doing there, and many hearts were touched. As I shared these things in Pastor Arian's church, he just stood there with tears streaming down his face. God moved mightily. I returned to Thailand with enough funding to begin work once again.

CHAPTER 23

WITH FUNDING IN hand, Deborah and I headed straight to the refugee camps along the Thai border. So many of the children were sick that the first thing we did was build a hospital. It was only bamboo walls and a grass roof, but we were able to stock it with much-needed medicine. In about six months we had built approximately five hundred houses for the refugees, seven hospitals, and a school for five thousand children. We fed between twenty-five and thirty thousand refugees daily before the money began to run out.

Pastor Arian contacted us to check on the situation, and I told him of our work, of everything we had been able to accomplish, but that we were almost out of money and the needs were still great. By the grace of

God he sent us another large offering. With this additional money we were able to continue our work.

OUR WORK EXPANDS IN CAMBODIA

Pastor Arian and his wife, with their tremendous hearts for the poor and lost, eventually came to visit us. At that time things were very dicey along the Thai border. Only God's protection kept us safe. We took them to the camps to see our feeding program. At one point I led them up a hill where we had built many of the refugee houses, and we were able to see the fighting.

He and his wife worked alongside us to feed the multitudes and distribute clothing, blankets, and medicine. Pastor Arian preached the gospel wherever we went; and when he preached, the Holy Spirit fell.

One day we visited a nearby army base. Pastor Arian preached powerfully to the generals and the leaders as I translated. Many of these battle-hardened men gave their lives to Christ as a result of his efforts. He felt strongly that he wanted an opportunity to lay hands on these men and pray for them, so we rented a large room in a nearby hotel. That night, as Pastor Arian began to preach, the Holy Spirit came in power. These three- and four-star generals began to fall under the power of the Spirit. Many of them stayed on the floor for hours, unable to get up.

Our work with the refugees continued, but now we had the attention of some high-ranking people in the military. One general who had been powerfully touched by the Holy Spirit asked to accompany me into the camps. I took him to the Kap Choeng District, to a refugee camp where about twenty thousand people were living. With us that day was the governor, who had also been powerfully touched in one of Pastor Arian's meetings. Many of the wives and children of the soldiers also wanted to see what we were doing. I had an opportunity to preach to them right there in the camp, and God came and touched them.

After seeing the plight of the refugees, this general asked for five thousand Bibles, which I was able to get for him. He gave one to every soldier under his command and ordered them to read one chapter a day. He told them that the Bible was God's holy book and whether or not they believed what was written there, they were to read it. As a result of his efforts, many of the soldiers gave their lives to Christ.

Generals, governors, soldiers, and refugees were coming into the kingdom in great numbers, and I was overjoyed. Even though I couldn't go into Cambodia at that time, God allowed me to minister to thousands of Cambodians in the camps. He came to me at one point with a very loving word that fortified my heart.

He said, "I know you have suffered for your country. I see your heart of compassion. And even though you have suffered, you have worked hard to lift the burden of suffering from others because of your great love for those I have brought to you. Because of your faithfulness and compassion, I am multiplying your efforts."

We had been away from our church in Phnom Penh for six months, and Deborah felt it was time for us to return. We gathered with our leaders to pray, and they too felt it was time for us to go. Because we were unsure if it was safe for me to return because of my government connections, Deborah went alone. She found the church stable and in good condition.

Two months later she contacted me and said it was OK for me to return to Phnom Penh. The government received me warmly, and we were able to increase our efforts to feed the poor. God's word to me that He would multiply my efforts became a reality in Phnom Penh just as it had in the camps along the Thai border.

Fruits of Obedience: The Sihanoukville Church

In the early 1990s, shortly after Deborah and I had returned to Cambodia, we began visiting prisons and hospitals. My goal was to take a team every Saturday. We would visit the prisons first and then the hospital. One day in the hospital I found myself ministering to a young man. I guessed him to be in his midtwenties. He was extremely thin. His doctor had told him he would soon be dead. God told me to spend some extra time with him.

He told us that his father had died and his mother was quite elderly. He had spent two years in the army, fighting in the jungles, and had contracted malaria. Many of his fellow soldiers had died of malaria, but he had been sent to the hospital. We laid hands on him and prayed for him and promised to return.

I felt prompted to go back the next morning with lots of fresh fruit. When I entered his room, he was sitting up in bed looking better than he had the night before. He was hungry, so I cut some fruit for him and fed him. God really touched my heart for this young man. I visited him every day for a week, feeding him, praying for him, and ministering to him.

At the end of a week's time he was ready to go home. His doctor insisted he was not strong enough to leave the hospital and that he needed surgery. I was able to make arrangements to take him back to the orphanage where we could care for him. At the time the orphanage was part of our house, so he came to live with me. I spent time with him every day and watched as God healed him. A month after we brought him home, he was well.

He was homesick and wanted to see his mother, so I made plans to drive him to Kampong Som Province, which is now known as the province of Sihanoukville. It was a seven-hour drive over poor roads and took us all day, but we finally arrived. His mother had not seen him in two years. Embracing, they clung to each other and wept.

I felt strongly that he was to plant a church there in his hometown. He had accepted Christ many years earlier, but when he went into the army, his faith had fallen by the wayside. Now, with God calling him back, he was ready to renew his faith. I stayed for three weeks to train him, and we were able to build a small church. It was basically a tent that could hold about twenty people.

When I returned a few months later, his church had grown to sixty-five people. They had outgrown their little tent, so we set about to build a larger structure with a restroom. He proved to be a strong pastor, and in a year's time his congregation had grown to one hundred twenty.

But God didn't stop there. The church continued to grow and grow. In two years they were out of that building and into a much larger one, and in five years they had outgrown the larger building. We began to pray and seek the Lord for provision of land, and eventually we found a beautiful piece of land beside the ocean.

God graciously provided the means, and in a year's time we had land. We began right away to construct the buildings God had shown us in a vision. Within twelve months we had three buildings on the property—a church that seated one thousand and two buildings for orphans that housed one hundred children each.

All of this began when I stopped to minister to a young man who lay dying in a hospital bed. In obedience to God's voice, I stopped and ministered, and God healed this young man and raised him up. Now hundreds have come to Christ in his church. Never underestimate the fruits of obedience.

AFTERWORD

SINCE THE EARLY 2000s our church building in Phnom Penh has been used as a conference and training center for Vietnamese pastors and leaders because they cannot meet freely in Vietnam. In 2010 healing evangelist and apostolic leader Randy Clark brought a team to our church to teach and minister to a contingent of Vietnamese pastors and leaders. It was a privilege to meet Dr. Clark. I could see clearly that God was touching his heart for the people of Cambodia and the work of our church. He returned to Cambodia to spend several days with me recording my story, which forms the basis of this book.

The Lord has blessed us mightily in Cambodia, but we suffered a great deal too. It was not just a physical war that wrenched Cambodia; a spiritual war also played itself out against the backdrop of the physical brutality. As God brought revival to Cambodia and it began to take hold, the attacks of the enemy increased. One hand worked to restore the country as another fought to tear it down.

In Cambodia there are strongholds of witchcraft that bring with them heavy darkness and oppression. If you don't know how to fight spiritual battles, you won't be able to withstand the warfare for very long. On the surface the church may appear to be doing well; we paid a heavy price, however, and people suffered greatly. I came under attack often, but God never failed to protect me.

As I look at the path of obedience that I learned to follow for the sake of God's kingdom, I think of the story of Saul's conversion from Acts 9. In that story God calls two people, Saul and Ananias, but gives them very different missions. He put a calling on Saul's life that became one of the greatest callings in the Bible. Ananias's mission seems small in comparison, but it wasn't small in the kingdom of God.

If you recall, Ananias tried to escape God's call because he was afraid—afraid he would suffer persecution if he tried to deal with Saul because Saul had done many evil things to the saints in Jerusalem. But God convinced him that this task set before him was of great importance, and so he obeyed. He was to lay hands on Saul and pray for his healing. When he did, Saul's eyes were opened, and Saul was renamed Paul and released as God's chosen instrument to carry the name of God before the Gentiles and their kings, and before the people of Israel.

Some are called to reach thousands, and others are called to reach only one person. Ananias was called to reach one person, Saul; and through Saul, God reached a nation and the world.

God can use anyone, and the tasks we are called to can be large or small. When we step out in faith, even when we are fearful, God is faithful. When we are not obedient to God's call, nothing happens; but when God calls and we obey, things happen. I have experienced these truths over and over again, and I know that if this is true for my life, then it is true for all believers.

When God first called me back to Cambodia in 1989, I was afraid. I had been imprisoned by the communists for many years, and I was an escaped prisoner, a fugitive. I didn't want to go back, and I resisted the call of God.

If we wait until every circumstance is just right in the natural, we will miss God's timing. His ways are not our ways, and His thoughts are not our thoughts. I have learned that if He comes to me at midnight and tells me to go, then I get up and go. I don't tell Him that I will wait until morning to go. I get up at midnight and I go. Some people think this is extreme, but I have learned to simply obey God.

Many times different missionary teams and groups have come to Cambodia to serve, but when they see the overwhelming needs, they tell me they can't do much because they don't have enough money and because the people of Cambodia don't have money either. They see the problems, but they don't see God. While I know that money is needed in the mission field, I also know that we shouldn't stop just because we don't have the money in hand. The way God builds His kingdom is different from the way we try to build His kingdom. I have learned to use the name of Jesus to build God's kingdom because all authority is in His name. With Jesus I can do anything; without Him I can do nothing.

Since 1994, for the last twenty-one years, we have prayed without ceasing for God to touch Cambodia and the world. Over the years God has brought many amazing men and women to Cambodia to help us rebuild our country. The Spirit of God has touched their hearts. Their call is no accident. They come because God speaks to their hearts. They come not only to Cambodia, but also to Thailand and Vietnam.

These are exciting times. God is revealing His manifest presence in Asia. We are seeing things today in these countries that have never been seen before. In the midst of great poverty and great need, God continues to advance His kingdom. Deborah and I, and the many others who serve faithfully and tirelessly alongside us, are privileged to be used by God in this corner of the world. Jesus is the desire of our hearts and the desire of the nations. I pray He is the desire of your heart as well. Almighty is His name!

BIBLIOGRAPHY

"Top Khmer Rouge Leaders' Trial Begins in Cambodia." Associated Press. November 20, 2011. Accessed October 1, 2015. http://news.yahoo.com/top-khmer -rouge-leaders-trial-begins-cambodia-022537174 .html.

Burke, Todd and DeAnn. *Anointed for Burial.* Plainfield, NJ: Bridge Logos, 1977.

"Cambodian Economy 2015." *CIA World Factbook.* Accessed October 1, 2015. http://www.theodora.com /wfbcurrent/cambodia/cambodia_economy.html.

"Cambodian Information Center." Cambodia.org.

"Cambodia." Christian and Missionary Alliance. Accessed October 1, 2015. http://www.cmalliance.org/field /cambodia.

Ferguson, Sarah. "Cambodia's Opposition Leader Says Australian Asylum Seeker Deal Will Fund Corruption." Australian Broadcasting Corporation. May 19, 2014. Accessed December 26, 2015. http:// www.abc.net.au/7.30/content/2014/s4007692.htm.

"Cambodia: Parliamentary Chamber: Constituent Assembly; Elections Held in 1993." Inter-Parliamentary Union. Accessed October 1, 2015. www.ipu.org/parline-e/reports/arc/2051_93.htm.

Chambers, John Whiteclay II, ed. 1999. *The Oxford Companion to American Military History.* New York: Oxford University Press Inc.

Sharp, Bruce. 1997. "Butchers on a Smaller Scale: Hun Sen and the Cambodian People's Party." Last modified 1998. Accessed October 1, 2015. http://www.mekong.net/cambodia/hun_sen1.htm.

——. May 2005. "Counting Hell." Last modified June 9, 2008. Accessed October 1, 2015. http://www.mekong.net/cambodia/deaths.htm.

——. "Landmines in Cambodia." Last modified June 2008. Accessed October 1, 2015. http://www.mekong.net/cambodia/mines.htm.

Stearns, Peter, ed. 2001. *The Encyclopedia of World History,* 6th ed. Boston: Houghton Mifflin Harcourt.

CONNECT WITH US!

**CHARISMA
HOUSE**

(Spiritual Growth)

f Facebook.com/CharismaHouse

🐦 @CharismaHouse

📷 Instagram.com/CharismaHouseBooks

SILOAM

(Health)

📍 Pinterest.com/CharismaHouse

REALMS

(Fiction)

f Facebook.com/RealmsFiction

SUBSCRIBE TODAY

Exclusive Content

Inspiring Messages

Encouraging Articles

Discovering Freedom

CHARISMA MEDIA

FREE NEWSLETTERS

to experience the power of the *Holy Spirit*

Charisma Magazine Newsletter
Get top-trending articles, Christian teachings, entertainment reviews, videos, and more.

Charisma News Weekly
Get the latest breaking news from an evangelical perspective every Monday.

SpiritLed Woman
Receive amazing stories, testimonies, and articles on marriage, family, prayer, and more.

New Man
Get articles and teaching about the realities of living in the world today as a man of faith.

3-in-1 Daily Devotionals
Find personal strength and encouragement with these devotionals, and begin your day with God's Word.

Sign up for Free at nl.charismamag.com